DON'T

JUST

PAY

TAXES

Divakar Vijayasarathy

DON'T

[JUST]

PAY
TAXES

HOW CONSCIOUS ENTREPRENEURS
PROFIT FROM TAXES

Forbes | Books

Published by Forbes Books, Charleston, South Carolina.
An imprint of Advantage Media Group.

Forbes Books is a registered trademark, and the Forbes Books colophon is a trademark of Forbes Media, LLC.

Printed in the United States of America.

10 9 8 7 6 5 4 3 2 1

ISBN: 979-8-88750-394-3 (Hardcover)
ISBN: 979-8-88750-395-0 (eBook)

Library of Congress Control Number: 2025908116

Cover design by Megan Elger.
Layout design by Ruthie Wood.
Author cover photo by Peter Hurley.

This custom publication is intended to provide accurate information and the opinions of the author in regard to the subject matter covered. It is sold with the understanding that the publisher, Forbes Books, is not engaged in rendering legal, financial, or professional services of any kind. If legal advice or other expert assistance is required, the reader is advised to seek the services of a competent professional.

Since 1917, Forbes has remained steadfast in its mission to serve as the defining voice of entrepreneurial capitalism. Forbes Books, launched in 2016 through a partnership with Advantage Media, furthers that aim by helping business and thought leaders bring their stories, passion, and knowledge to the forefront in custom books. Opinions expressed by Forbes Books authors are their own. To be considered for publication, please visit **books.Forbes.com**.

12-09-2025 12:46

To the man who helped me in my first step on this earth

To the man who made me whatever I am and whatever I wish to be

To the man who taught me how to dream and more importantly to achieve them

To the man who inspired me to see hurdles as challenges and obstacles as opportunities

To the man who instilled in me the insatiable desire for success and excellence

To the man who saw the world through my eyes for the best part of his parenthood

To the man who never said "No" to me in his entire life

To the man who taught me the meaning of the term sacrifice and selflessness

To the man whose last few words are always loud in my ears

Dad, I really miss you in my life

I am sure, but for your wishes and blessings, I would never have been whatever I am

Thanks a lot Dad for whatever you have been, this humble effort is entirely dedicated to you

August 2010

CONTENTS

INTRODUCTION

> *CHILDREN ARE THE LIVING MESSAGES WE SEND*
> *TO A TIME WE MAY NOT SEE.*
> *—JOHN F. KENNEDY*

Dear fellow traveler,

I spend my days discussing the intricacies and strategies of taxation, both in my native country, India, and internationally. At night I tell my children bedtime stories, which are purposefully focused on the reality of my daily life. Building a successful business as a global tax advisor has been challenging, to say the least. As I overcame the false starts, setbacks, and failures, and developed the philosophy that I will be discussing in this book, I realized that what I was learning from life was much more profound and relevant than what the academy had taught me. Gradually, I even began losing faith in the structured education my children were receiving.

"Let's pull the kids out of school," I told my wife, Kavitha.

She was perplexed but responded forcefully, something like "That's not going to happen!"

Her reply was not surprising, given her conservative background. I devised an alternate plan in which we would not homeschool the kids, but I would engage with them during bedtime in a casual conversation, that in my mind was structured to formally train them. Starting when the older one was five or six, I began making notes of every encounter and experience during my day that provided material for instructive bedtime stories. Also, while reading books, I would mark a *K* (for kids' stories) and note the page number of a conversation starter for that night. Over time, the conversations not only became an integral part of our lives and their education; I realized that my lovely kids were educating me in return with their questions. I couldn't have asked for better tutors in my life than my kids. I owe much of my intellectual curiosity and consequent clarity to them. Their fundamental and innocent questions often challenged my intellect. Their questions were simple, but profound and deep. As Albert Einstein once said, "It takes a genius to simplify." I would add this: "Children are born geniuses awaiting adulteration by the planet."

Whenever I used a new term in these bedtime stories such as *taxation, evasion, legislation*, etc., I would be bombarded with Socratic-style questioning—simple, yet deeply probing. My clients are always asking, "How can I reduce my tax liability?" But no one asked me, "Why should I pay taxes?" until my young son brought up that question:

Sanjay (son): Appa [father], I earn and get paid for my efforts, so why should I pay the government?

Me: The government helps us earn money by building the roads we use to go to the office, the airports we use for traveling for work, and the police and military that keep us safe while we're doing that.

Sanjay: I understand, but who decides how my money is spent? Even when you give us pocket money, you ask us for an accounting.

Me: The ruling government decides how the money is spent, and the finance minister of the country gives a yearly statement. It's called the Union Budget of India.

Sanjay: Appa, what if I don't like how they spend my money? Can I get it back?

Me: Sorry, no.

Sanjana (daughter): But why? That isn't fair. I worked hard for it, and I should have a say in how it's spent.

Me: I agree. And if you're unhappy with the government's way of spending, you can vote for a different government in the next elections.

Sanjay: When do elections come?

Me: Once every five years [in India].

Sanjana: So, until then, they can do whatever they want?

Me: Hmm … yes, you are right.

Sanjay: That is totally wrong. I will not accept this.

Sanjana: If I buy a book on Amazon, and it's torn, I can return it. But if the huge amount of tax I pay is not used properly, I must keep quiet. That is totally unfair.

Me: I agree, but tell me, if every citizen had a say in how their tax money was spent, would we ever agree on anything?

Sanjay: Is this how it happens in all countries?

Me: To my knowledge, this is how it happens in democracies. However, I promise to read more about this, and I will come back to you tomorrow. Good night now. I love you both.

Thanks to conversations like these, I started researching public spending by governments around the world and throughout history. It added flavor and perspective to my journey of trying to understand the mysterious world of taxation, its significant players, and how it can be improved to benefit everyone, especially our children.

My Career Journey

You might say I am an accidental accountant who initially wanted to be a doctor. In actuality, landing in the field of accounting was just a stop on my way to being an entrepreneur. In 2004, I qualified as a public accountant, India's equivalent of passing the CPA exam if you are in the United States. India's financial and tax regulations are so complicated that the exam has a pass percentage of less than 0.5%. Being among the top-tier qualifiers, I had access to the best placements and took a well-paying management job with one of India's largest public sector companies in the petroleum industry. But I couldn't bear sitting around in an organization stultified by government bureaucracy. When I quit after only 25 days, before I could even receive my first paycheck, I struggled for a few months to find my purpose in life. I left my large coastal city, Chennai, to join a multibillion-dollar manufacturing company for a great job but left it about three months later to return home, where my father was ailing. I then joined a top bank in Chennai, Kotak Mahindra Bank, taking a 70% salary cut. The work was interesting, and I stayed a little over a year before moving up to an international bank. My salary increased fourfold at Citibank, where I headed risk management in two regions of southern and eastern India—an area with a larger population than the United States—by age 25. I left after seven months.

I quit four jobs because I didn't fit the corporate mold and found the ambience stifling, even when I enjoyed the work. At Citibank, for example, my team's job was to scrutinize loans of $1 million to $10 million for small and midsize organizations. Calculating the ideal amount of risk was interesting, but I'm personally more oriented toward taking risks than managing and controlling risks. What I needed was my own lab where I could use my thought process to experiment, take on challenges, and test my ideas. Out of this personal need for independence and freedom, I launched DVS Advisors in 2007, coincidentally on my 26th birthday.

The culture in India is such that family obligations are paramount. My folks were looking out for a suitable bride so they could arrange a marriage for me. I had taken jobs and avoided marriage because I wanted my father to know his son was secure. By 2007, my dad had passed away, and I explained to my older brother that I was uncomfortable in the corporate world. "Okay, fine. Quit and do whatever you want," he said, giving me permission to leave a secure job despite our commitment to provide family support.

Over the next 18 years, I took many risks to extend my business with new ventures. Some lost money and had to be shut down. I came close to bankruptcy three times, but the journey on the whole was enriching, rewarding, and above all, fulfilling. Now, after putting radical business experimentation on hold for a few years and consolidating DVS Advisors in a growth mode, I want to share what has made the firm unique: we help entrepreneurs and governments profit from taxes. I'll explain in the pages ahead why I built a business around taxation and how I learned to understand it differently than most people and companies do.

> We help entrepreneurs and governments profit from taxes.

Taxation and Alignment

This book is meant to help business owners, or really anyone who pays taxes, devise strategies that align with the tax-regimes and regulations imposed by governments. It can help those who levy taxes devise suitable policies to promote society's interests. I also hope that students who aim to be entrepreneurs or policymakers will read this book and start looking at the imposition of taxation as more of a behavioral science than simply a fiscal levy. This idea of looking at tax as profit, not as liability or burden, requires a complete shift in our thinking. I ask readers to allow me to walk them through my business journey in the first part of the book so they can see for themselves what inspired my ideas about taxation. The second part discusses the strategies, and how they can be integrated into business plans or applied by policymakers. If these strategies were easy to imagine and apply, they would be much more widely adopted than they are. The final third explores how to solve the challenges that keep us from seeing or trusting in tax alignment.

If you are an entrepreneur, the subject of taxation tends to be a source of fear. People fear learning how much they owe, especially when they receive a surprise assessment or demand letter. Being able to look at the tax collector, not as someone who is out there to exploit you, can be liberating. The same perspective on tax collection, if understood and embraced by policymakers, could have a profound impact on our world. Policymakers viewing their citizens as partners in progress could find more ways to use the carrot rather than the stick—the threat of penalties and fines—to allocate resources and align public behavior.

This book is primarily aimed at entrepreneurs and business leaders seeking to transform their approach to taxation. While our focus is on business strategies, we recognize that for many entrepreneurs, personal and business finances are closely intertwined. Therefore, we'll also touch on personal tax considerations as they relate to entrepreneurship and business decision-making. By the end of this book, you'll have a comprehensive understanding of how to align your business—and by extension, your personal financial goals—with broader societal needs through strategic tax planning.

What I'm sharing are truths that have always been there for anyone who was able and willing to see them. It's just that we as a society have not asked the right questions for which the regulations have always had answers. I'm not here to lobby or influence any regulator. The regulators have done the thinking part. The entrepreneurs will now have to do the asking part, and our job at DVS Advisors has been to ask the right questions about the regulation (not to the regulator) on their behalf and to execute what the regulator wants. As we began viewing the world through this prism, our work naturally expanded—clients from different geographies, cultures, and regulatory systems found resonance in what we had to offer. Over time, and across more than 40 jurisdictions, a quiet but powerful truth revealed itself: what entrepreneurs and policymakers ultimately seek is not all that different. The real challenge lies not in intent, but in language—how they understand and speak to one another.

This book is a journey into that realization. It is not built on abstraction, but on lived patterns—experiences that have repeated often enough to feel foundational. These insights may not claim to be universal truths, but they have been enduringly true in my world.

So, let's begin the journey.

Divakar Vijayasarathy

PART I

Inspiration

CHAPTER 1

Despair Turned to Innovation—*Learning by Launching and Almost Losing a Firm*

[WHEN BUSINESS GOALS AND NATIONAL
OBJECTIVES ALIGN, TAXES BECOME PROFITS.]

I launched a firm focused on international tax issues the year before the Great Recession of 2008, but I was already having my own financial crisis when the world economy nosedived. I was not on a solid financial footing to start with because my childhood was a riches-to-rags story. Living amid slums, my father ran a successful art academy until he suddenly couldn't, as he became blind as I was entering my teenage years. My older brother and I pitched in to support the family, and we shared a home in which I converted a small attic into a humble workspace after starting DVS Advisors. Accounting firms in India are typically named after the proprietor, but since Divakar Vijayasarathy is such a long name, I shortened it to three initials. Soon after the business got going, I married and was expecting our child, so I was delighted when DVS obtained a contract that appeared large enough to change my life financially. I felt DVS had arrived—until we sent our first invoice to the client in Africa after 30 days.

When the client's CFO informed me that his country's law required 30% to be withheld for taxes, I took that as an unfortunate learning experience. But bad turned to worse when he explained that his country had no mechanism to provide a withholding certificate, meaning we would owe an additional 40% in taxes back in India. 70% of my revenue would be lost to taxes. Also, he forgot to mention, before we signed the contract, that it might take six months to pay us because converting the local currency in his company bank account for foreign exchange would take a low-priority route through the country's central bank. We ended up abandoning the contract and not being paid, but for a time we had to continue to pay the personnel we had hired to get the job done. My company was in serious jeopardy of failing at that point.

> 70% of my revenue would be lost to taxes.

Amid the shock and disappointment, I learned a lesson that revenue is not confirmed until it's money in the bank. But I also had a revelation. Entrepreneurs are trained to think, *If it's a problem for me, it's a problem for everyone (or at least a lot of others)*, meaning there's an opportunity in solving the problem. I set out to learn everything I could about taxation law, including why and how taxation started. One Sunday morning, I was reading about Jizya, a tax Muslim leaders levied many centuries ago on non-Muslims. Families providing military service could be exempt. The fascinating takeaway for me was that the tax was not so much a fee as it was a penalty for noncompliance in that region—a tool for the government to align public behavior. My entire perspective on taxation changed, and I started looking at regulations in a different way (which we will discuss further in chapter 3).

The Path to Alignment

I founded DVS coincidentally on my 26th birthday after trying a series of four corporate jobs. I was fully aware that I didn't have a clue what I would do with the new company, but I was clear on what I would not do. I was certified as a public accountant and had been teaching about taxation, but I was not interested in creating a conventional accounting firm and doing typical work on tax compliance. I decided to focus on international tax issues because it was new to me, which made it stimulating and invigorating. The field calls for intellectual rigor because it requires understanding the convergence of taxation and geopolitics. As in the United States, where tax laws run a few thousand pages, India's tax laws are notoriously complex and dynamic.

In my first few years as an accountant, keeping up with India's many tax law amendments every year was an interesting challenge. I'm an early riser, so in 2004 I took a side job from 6:15 a.m. to 8:30 a.m. teaching at a professional institute where students train to become accountants and prepare for the certification exam. I was the teacher but had to be constantly learning myself, and I became curious about why these amendments were made and what their effects were. This curiosity developed into a philosophy of how tax systems around the world reward us when we align our actions with the priorities of the government. In practice, this means asking the right questions of the law and then profiting by giving the regulators what they want.

To start DVS, I registered a business name, got approval from the accounting regulators, and created a bank account. I would tell you that I then rented offices and hired a full staff ... if it were an ideal world. At first, I ran my business alone out of the ground-floor room that I shared with my mom in my brother's house, using the

Acer laptop computer I had bought on an installment plan while working for Citibank. I still had three installment payments due. But after a few months, I hired my first employee, an office boy, and it was time to move up … to the attic. Each month that followed, we accomplished a milestone: clearing junk out of the storage space to make an office, repairing the window that wouldn't open, redoing the washroom, painting. I was ashamed to let clients see the office, so we had only one visitor, the *chaiwallah*, a guy who would come by on a bicycle each day with a big flask of tea.

After several months, a friend from my former job at the bank joined my firm as a partner, and we got an accounting contract from an American hedge fund. We recruited about 50 people to fulfill this contract, mostly new accountants I met through my teaching. To accommodate the new staff, my brother gave me money to fix up a house I had bought with a mortgage when I was working for Citibank. Just as the project was supposed to begin operations in September 2008, Lehman Brothers collapsed, and our American client emailed us to cancel our contract. That was a low point in my entrepreneurial journey. My partner emailed me, saying that he needed a steady job and would go back to the bank. I was planning a honeymoon in Paris. But my firm was obligated to keep all those new employees on for three months, so I scrambled to get money to pay them. I sold the house, borrowed additional money, and shifted the honeymoon from Paris to a neighboring state, Kerala. (I finally managed to take Kavitha to Paris in 2024.)

Bringing Family on the Journey

I have not insulated my family from the ups and downs of my business ventures. I took the wise advice of a friend who told me, "Don't just tell them the good things that happen. Be vulnerable in front of your kids. Tell them you are going through a financial challenge. Tell them you feel disturbed. Tell them you're volatile." My wife and kids are very much part of the journey, including the decisions we make and the challenges we go through. These are simply parts of life. As I mentioned earlier, I shared my experiences with my kids as bedtime stories, and these included the challenges we faced and the mistakes we made at work. The lesson I was imparting was that making mistakes is fine, but not learning from them is a crime. I don't just say, "I've made a mistake." I want to reflect on those mistakes to gain a deeper understanding of what happened and why it happened. By understanding our blind spots, we can evolve and grow. As a reader, I hope you will benefit both from what I learned personally and from your own reflection on society's insular view of taxation.

Going after my entrepreneurial dream, building a company with a presence in four countries and partners in over 100 countries, has required bringing my family along on a difficult journey. Kavitha is not only a great mother but also co-founder and chief operating officer of DVS. She has masterminded our various moves, including my collection of antique furniture and statues, and set up our home seven times in the past nine years. Amid the moves, the children occasionally had to live out of hotels and had to change schools and make new friends, but they have been more than accommodating. Every Sunday morning at 11:00 a.m. we have a one-hour meeting of the immediate family forum, which we call "the Explorers." We elect a moderator to serve for 12 weeks. We start our discussion with one word that depicts our state of mind. If it is *gratitude*, for example, we discuss the best moment that happened to us in the past week was, whom we are grateful for, and what they did for us that week. Then we have a list of four commitments, encompassing personal, academic, community, and family.

Each family member takes on one of each commitment for the week. The next Sunday we come back and share our achievements, earning points for each of the achievements. The rest of the hour is filled with a presentation. For example, I have a long presentation that I have broken into pieces of four or five slides each on the 2017 best-selling book *Principles*, by Ray Dalio, which is about how to get the life and work you want. My 13-year-old made a presentation on what it takes to achieve one of her goals, which is getting into the Oxford University law school.

THE CLARITY OF CHILDREN

After several years of bedtime discussions with my children about everything I see and experience at work and in life, they have matured into excellent sounding boards. They are like a board of directors with less baggage and more clarity, seeing things I miss. In fact, I have brought one of them into my office to sit and observe at a distance as I interviewed recruits or discussed trying something new. Their feedback is unbiased, and instead of rationalizing decisions based on reading a résumé as an executive would do, their young brains can sense authenticity and the difference between fake and genuine job candidates. And I am not just boasting about my kids. Wherever I go, if I have a chance to talk to children about what I am reading or to read together with them, I find they ask excellent questions that make me think, and I enjoy learning from them.

A Big Insight on a Tiny Island

About halfway through my first year as an entrepreneur, I traveled to Mauritius for about a week to advise a client on a cross-border tax-structuring transaction. The Indian government back then was encouraging Americans to invest in India via Mauritius, an Indian Ocean island country. The promise was tax savings, but necessary knowledge about the correct structuring was not widespread or available through an online search back then. Investors would not want to take chances with India's aggressive tax bureaucracy, which was incentivized to make large cross-border tax demands. India originates more than half the cases globally on tax litigation and international tax. The target companies can challenge the demands, but they would be legally required to pay a 20% to 50% deposit unless they could win a stay, which would require getting a hearing in notoriously slow and backlogged courts.

Because the only flights between my home city of Chennai and Mauritius were on Tuesdays, I had to stay there for a week. I passed my time visiting with the hundred-plus law firms and accounting firms that had small storefronts in Mauritius. I was surprised to learn that one small firm could be generating multimillion-dollar annual revenue. Back in India, midsize firms might make $200,000 or, if they were fortunate, $300,000. I realized that the disparity in revenue was a result of India's public accountants having a lack of freedom under our extensive code of conduct to engage in multinational partnerships. The firms in Mauritius told me they had partner offices in France, the United States, and other countries that would both do part of their work and source clients for them. Mauritius had long been colonized by France and then Britain, so it has those cultural and language ties. And since it became independent in 1968, Mauritius has developed into a friendly hub for investment, particularly in India and Africa. I couldn't replicate the business model I was seeing there because, after studying so hard to pass probably the toughest professional exam in India, I was chained by hundreds of pages of regulations telling me what I couldn't do. Arriving back home, I surrendered my license to be a public accountant. I didn't see it as a big decision at the time, but it was a career turning point because it shut off options that I may have considered for my family's financial security, but ultimately would not have personally enjoyed.

The Cross-Border Minefield

In the African country where my tax-withholding nightmare happened, the client was buying very expensive mining equipment from South Asia. It was cheaper to ship the equipment all the way around southern Africa than to buy it in Africa, after considering how much they could deploy the equipment and what they could charge mine owners who did not wish to invest in their own equipment. The client, in turn, outsourced to DVS the job of structuring the transaction and implementing and maintaining that structure. At the time, our world did not have reliable, standardized, and internationally recognized methods of identifying bank accounts for electronic transfers of money across borders. It took research and patience to move the money involved in cross-border contracts. Even now, we must structure transactions to lose as little as possible on exchange rates, commissions, and bank charges.

For readers who may not be familiar, here is some brief background on structuring international transactions. You are no doubt aware that companies can often save money if they buy, lease, or hire out goods and services from another country. In the process, they may need outside expertise to ensure that the contract complies with laws in all jurisdictions involved, that money is moved effectively, and that taxes are not overpaid or underpaid. Anyone who travels overseas knows what a headache it can be just researching logistics, even something as simple as whether to buy a mobile data plan at home or at their destination. But entrepreneurs willing to take on substantially greater logistical challenges can profit from the cost arbitrage in which one business offers to save another money by scouting out a bargain, often resulting from a crisis or hardship in another region.

Tax as Profit

A former member of one of America's big three global management consulting firms was my first large international tax client. He was moving from Italy to India and paid my company INR 1 million to structure a transaction. In today's US dollars, he paid about $12,000, of which I would clear about $3,000 as my fee. Finally, I could buy a car! I spent my entire proceeds to obtain a silver Škoda Octavia, the same model and color a former boss had bought in his 25th year of being an accountant. I hadn't been able to qualify for a car loan because I'd just started my business. But once I had a car, I could refinance it and use the loan money to pay my business bills. This scheme gave me confidence. I felt successful because I could make a purchase in my first year that my boss had made in his 25th year. As I recall this story 18 years later, DVS Advisors has expanded globally with over 17,000 clients.

The success stems from our viewing tax as an opportunity and not as a cost. While every tax law must spell out how it will be administered, collected, and enforced, its core is devoted to offering incentives to avoid paying that tax. That reward is the opportunity to profit. Some readers might see this book mostly as a guide to help them profit from a better understanding of taxes, but I hope to convince you there are broader benefits. Tax alignment can bring huge changes.

Consider this recent example from India, where the government had a program subsidizing cooking gas for pretty much anyone in the entire population of about 1.4 billion people. The policy was written so the government could not refuse requests for a household allocation of several liquefied petroleum gas fuel cylinders per year. In 2015, Prime Minister Narendra Modi launched a "Give It Up" campaign basically asking people to think about whether they needed the subsidy. Domestic and international politics prevented Modi from targeting the subsidy more directly, but he presented the option of surrendering the subsidy as a way of contributing to India's general welfare. More than 10 million households decided they could afford to pay for their own cooking gas, freeing up funds to help reshape the program to benefit over 15 million poor households. The people who decided to forgo the subsidy did so because they felt aligned with the government's vision of spending the money where it was needed.

This idea that taxes enable good things to happen requires policymakers to communicate a vision but also to give up some control. The more common approach for leaders is to use fear to enforce compliant behavior. When entrepreneurs feel constrained by the tax policies where they live or do business, they can spend money pushing back, lobbying for changes and loopholes, or they can learn how to make money, aligning with the vision policymakers are communicating.

Connecting the Dots

I am a trained artist who, when I was young, held two art exhibitions of my drawings and oil paintings—and let me explain how that experience is relevant to our subject of taxation strategy. As background, I come from a family of artists. My dad expanded the art institute founded by his father to train about 3,000 students per year at the peak of his career, before his vision failed. When Dad's blindness took away his ability to manage the business, we still wanted to fulfill our commitment to the students already in the three-year program. I was just becoming a teenager but had to help manage the business for a couple of years before we could shut it down. That experience had a profound impact on my psyche, as I realized, *Every bad phase shall pass.* With my brother and me still in school, Dad sustained us financially by trading in the stock market, investing based on what he learned from having my mom read the newspapers to him.

What we learned from producing art was akin to what the business guru Stephen R. Covey dubbed "Habit 2": "Begin with the End in Mind." We start our artwork with the outline, envisioning the entire picture, and then we start connecting. The outline is not necessarily made up of lines and can be dots. Connecting the dots produces the complete picture. When I started connecting the dots in the vast, complex panorama that is taxation, I started to see why the levies are so different from one country to another. Now the picture has become so familiar in my mind that I can sense the direction and complexion of an area's tax laws just by driving down its roads.

It may seem like an unlikely connection, but motorists' behavior reflects anxiety levels, which correlate with economic factors. In lower-income countries with high anxiety levels among residents, you'll notice motorists creeping forward past the stop line. The same countries have a smaller tax base, requiring higher tax rates to compensate, higher official corruption, and bureaucratic inefficiencies. Countries where drivers patiently wait in traffic tend to have higher per capita gross domestic product (GDP), a higher tax-to-GDP ratio, and robust social security systems. The drivers' orderly conduct signifies lower anxiety levels, as citizens trust the state to take care of them. Their adherence to traffic rules may mean it takes them a bit longer to travel the same distance, but this minor inconvenience is balanced by their having greater trust in others and ample opportunities to channel their competitive spirit into more productive avenues.

How to Feel Empowered, Not Cheated

The intent and purpose of this book is to open the minds of readers to the positive aspects of taxation, as difficult as that concept may be to embrace. I believe the ideas here are simple to understand, and that is because they were inspired by the innocent questions of my children. Please note that I cite occasional examples from India because they are familiar to me, not because I am demonizing my homeland's regulators. India's tax regulations have progressed in the decade and a half since my eye-opening trip to Mauritius, but they reflect a reality often challenging to cross-border entrepreneurs everywhere: policymakers focus on their country's internal needs and issues more than on understanding external factors that shape international commerce. As a result, optimal tax strategy should align business and personal interests with government priorities.

> Optimal tax strategy should align business and personal interests with government priorities.

The first third of the book explains how to understand and profit from this reality. We'll look back at the history and purposes of taxes and how they aim to affect public behavior with what I call the three Ps of alignment: **priority, paranoia, and prohibition**. The second third of the book drills down into strategies of alignment available to businesses, individuals, and society. The final third addresses the real-world challenges to tax alignment, which often live in our own heads whether we are accountants, entrepreneurs, policymakers, or ordinary taxpayers. I wrap up the book with a positive vision for returning taxation to its original purposes and envision a future of possibilities.

The devastating experience in Africa that endangered my company's future left me feeling robbed by taxation, but it also resulted in clarity about how I could profit from aligning with governmental priorities. **I went from feeling cheated to feeling empowered.** By nature, I enjoy seeking, learning, and sharing, which has compelled me to dig deeper into this alignment concept and whether it has applications beyond personal or business profit. The next chapter explores the realities and the possibilities of extending the principle of alignment in society to better meet people's needs and expectations.

CHAPTER 2

Changing Your Mindset–
Seeing Tax as Profit

[

TAX IS NOT ABOUT ENFORCEMENT,

IT'S ABOUT INTENT.

]

My 11-year-old son asked me a question: "Dad, aren't humans the only species who need to pay to exist on the planet?" It's so true. What's also true is that in every society, we pay differently and get different rewards in return. The rules of taxation and the surrounding politics define our world and mark the differences between nations. Let's look at some examples.

In China, the government poured resources into lifting people out of poverty, transforming their lives, and urbanizing neighborhoods, but in the process took them out of the world they knew.

In India, by a common measure, the standard of living is low: the GDP per capita was US$2,481 in 2023 compared with $82,769 in the United States, according to the World Bank.[1] Less than 5% of India's taxpayer population is obligated to pay income tax. Agricultural income is not taxed, which exempts about two-thirds of the population, and others are exempted because their wages are so low. But $250 a month is a good income for someone to exist with dignity in the country. In my home state of Tamil Nadu, you can get a large meal for as little as five cents. A value-added tax on goods and services ensures that consumption helps fund the government. India doesn't have a substantial social security budget, but it also doesn't have a substantial homelessness problem. A strong sense of charity and community within the population ensures that even the poor have homes in India.

In the United States, the national wealth has not kept homelessness and poverty from plaguing cities despite a progressive rate system for personal income taxes. Corporate tax rates are kept relatively low compared with personal tax rates, as in most capitalistic societies. The defensible premise is that corporate income tax is a tax on efficiency and productivity, which the government should be rewarding, not discouraging.

Tax revenue as a percentage of GDP varies widely by country, from over 40% in Scandinavia and France to less than 2% in Kuwait by some measures. The numbers are reported inconsistently, but generally the larger and more developed nations have a tax-to-GDP ratio of 25% to 35%, at least double what we see in India and emerging markets. Some may dismiss the ratio as just another dry economic statistic, but it profoundly reflects cultural values and how we live. The higher the percentage of tax revenue to GDP, the

---

1   "GDP per Capita (Current US$)," World Bank national accounts data and OECD National Accounts data files; accessed June 8, 2024, https://data.worldbank.org/indicator/ny.gdp.pcap.cd.

more decisions the government is taking away from the people. This delegation of authority passes as a type of freedom for some people, with those high-taxed Nordic people famously topping the United Nations' World Happiness Report. Other societies don't see it as freedom—

> The higher the percentage of tax revenue to GDP, the more decisions the government is taking away from the people.

they see a big daddy or strict nanny dictating how they should live and what they should go after in life.

Also ranking very high on the happiness list is Bhutan, a very small Buddhist country that restricts tourism and insulates itself from the contamination of capitalistic beliefs. A former prime minister of Bhutan explained to me that his culture maintains that anyone who defines happiness or success in monetary terms doesn't understand happiness or success.

These societal differences create the broader context within which we must consider our premise of tax alignment. Some of us must change our mindset more than others to enjoy the freedom of taking control of our lives and businesses by aligning them with governmental tax systems.

Who Decides Where Taxes Go?

Taxation has been demonized throughout history as a method by which the ruler fleeces the subjects, but how accurate is that view? As a modern society creates value, measured in GDP, the government takes a share, but much of that is in turn distributed to citizens and various social institutions. How this happens varies by jurisdiction, but it is hard to imagine a government anywhere that is not funneling money into social safety net programs, such as feeding the poor. Some cash transfers go directly to citizens through pension and welfare programs, and some go to not-for-profit organizations, which include some but not all hospitals, clinics, and nursing homes or educational institutions. The entire challenge behind tax laws is about who gets a say on this allocation of capital. Governments inevitably fall short of being a fair and efficient allocator of capital, and there is always a conflict between taxpayers and the regulators over capital allocation. **This conflict is not so much about tax rates as it is about control,** a distinction we see in prominent instances of philanthropy. For example, the American billionaire Warren Buffett pledged in 2006 to gradually give all his Berkshire Hathaway stock to philanthropic foundations. In 2010, Microsoft founder Bill Gates joined Buffett in a campaign called "The Giving Pledge" to encourage billionaires around the world to contribute at least 50% of their wealth to charity. Buffett famously said that spending more than 1% of his stock certificates on himself and his family would not enhance their happiness or well-being, but the remaining 99% could have a huge effect on the health and welfare of others. Buffett and Gates went on to donate billions of dollars to charity and got many tycoons to sign on to the 50% pledge.

> Governments inevitably fall short of being a fair and efficient allocator of capital, and there is always a conflict between taxpayers and the regulators over capital allocation.

Can you imagine Buffett and Gates, instead of creating a pledge, paying 50% tax voluntarily? Would any of them have signed on? If the US government levied a flat 50% tax on billionaires, how many would flee the country? Examples abound of wealthy people relocating from high-tax jurisdictions. Buffett's pledge involved philanthropy because it provided him a degree of control over how his charitable giving would be allocated. **This idea that "we the people" can be more efficient or fair than government at capital allocation is universal** and hardly limited to billionaires or millionaires. In chapter 1 we saw how India, a developing country, subsidized cooking gas with a ration to every family, rich or poor. When a new prime minister asked people who didn't need the subsidy to voluntarily surrender it, millions did so, not just as a matter of pride but because they welcomed having the power to decide whether they deserved it. **Anytime control shifts from the government to the taxpayer, it boosts morale.**

At a local level, consider what could happen to a large plot of undeveloped land. The city government might want to see a developer come in and build housing, a shopping center, or offices to generate tax revenue. Neighbors might prefer open space, such as a community park, but to achieve that goal, they would have to organize a substantial political pressure campaign. Suppose the government agrees to support a park, but only by offering to match private contributions or give tax credits to incentivize donors. What the government has done, essentially, is to impose a choice between a giving pledge or passive acceptance of whatever development ensues on that vacant land. Maybe the residents would get better police and fire protection from the revenue windfall resulting from the development, or maybe they would get only higher-paid city bureaucrats. If residents succeeded in raising money for a park, however, donors would pocket the tax credits, and residents would enjoy the new park even more because they controlled the outcome.

Allocation of Scarce Resources

The opportunity to use tax alignment as an alternative to top-down mandates can be seen clearly when societies are forced to allocate natural resources. An example involves the battles over water rights in the US Southwest after years of drought and climate change. The Colorado River provides water to more than 40 million people[2] under a century-old agreement that allocates significantly more supply than currently exists, while demand increases because too many people planted lawns and water-intensive crops in a sunny but arid region.[3] Growing cities such as Las Vegas and Phoenix and their suburbs are competing with farmers and ranchers for water, so ideally everyone would find ways to conserve. Voluntary agreements with California, Nevada, and Arizona have helped to some extent, but not enough.[4]

Government attempts to mandate even greater conservation inevitably would get dragged into long court battles, and rely on forcing the agriculture industry to spend dearly on new technology for irrigation. That spending would drive up food prices domestically and make the country less competitive internationally. Another option is to wait for supply and demand to make water more costly, displeasing everyone. A situation like this with hard choices is an opportunity for government to use tax policy to align people's interests. Federal, state, and local governments essentially pay people to save water. For example, a 2022 California law exempts from the state income tax, money that residents

2   Ella Nilsen and Rachel Ramirez, "'The Brink of Disaster': 2023 Is a Critical Year for the Colorado River as Reservoirs Sink Toward 'Dead Pool,'" CNN, December 30, 2022, https://edition.cnn.com/2022/12/30/us/colorado-river-lake-mead-drought-2023-climate/index.html.

3   Elizabeth Weise and Trevor Hughes, "'Dead Pool' Approaches: Western Water Crisis Looms as California Complicates Critical Water Deal," USA Today, February 2, 2023, updated February 12, 2023, https://www.usatoday.com/story/news/2023/02/02/colorado-river-compact-water-crisis-california-plan-explained/11170739002.

4   Julia Jacobo and Stephanie Ebbs, "States Dependent on Colorado River Required to Conserve Unprecedented Amount of Water in Deal," ABC News, May 22, 2023, https://abcnews.go.com/US/states-dependent-colorado-river-required-conserve-unprecedented-amount/story?id=99509575.

receive to replace their lawns with desert landscaping.[5] The six-year program aligned state tax law with an increasingly popular response to a historic drought. More broadly, the US government decided in November 2021 to put billions of dollars into funding water conservation, recycling projects and improving watershed management.[6] The federal initiative encourages hundreds of local quasi-governmental or independent agencies to align with conservation goals. The short-term outcome of these initiatives is often visible, at least in certain regions to individuals who are managing water costs or seeing their neighbors' front yards transformed but measuring the broader long-term impact will take years.

An example from India illustrates the difficulty of implementing an incentive across a diverse country. At the end of 2022, the Indian government announced a generous national financial assistance program intended to accelerate the growth of solar energy produced from grid-connected household rooftop installations. Many state governments offered related subsidies, but participation was concentrated in a few states, particularly Gujarat, and lacking. The environmental news website Down to Earth (India edition) reported that there was no definitive count of households installing rooftop solar, but that the Delhi-based think tank Centre for Science and Environment estimated it was below one million, far short of the renewable energy program's goal. Analysts blamed the complex and time-consuming

---

5   "California Is Making It Cheaper to Replace Your Lawn to Save Water and Save Money," State of California, September 28, 2022, https://www.gov. ca.gov/2022/09/28/california-is-making-it-cheaper-to-replace-your-lawn-to-save-water-and-save-money.

6   Peter Gleick, Amanda Bielawski, and Heather Cooley, "The US Infrastructure Plan: Water Components," Pacific Institute, accessed August 7, 2023, https://pacinst.org/the-u-s-infrastructure-plan-water-components.

installation process, bureaucratic delays, and a lack of awareness among potential beneficiaries.[7]

Paying for Shared Services

All governments are service providers, but how they collect the revenue to pay for those services varies. Dubai, the Persian Gulf coastal city in the United Arab Emirates (UAE), is renowned as a tax haven, which means it attracts entrepreneurs who have the typical disdain for taxes. The common mindset is "I earn more because of my efficiency, and the government should not feast on my efficiency." What these entrepreneurs quickly learn is that nothing in the UAE is free. There is a fee for everything, from owning a company, to using the roads, to parking in what appears to be wide-open space. The government maintains enticing public parks but charges small usage fees. If the government failed to deliver, it would not collect its fees. The clear message from this system is that being in a tax haven results in a higher cost of living but offers the satisfaction of getting what you pay for. The fee system in Dubai is like a hotel that charges separate fees for use of its pool, spa, and other services, in contrast with those hotels that charge a "resort fee" even if a guest never uses those facilities. **With no personal income tax, but a value-added tax on all goods and services, Dubai has shifted control from the regulator to the regulated.** The efficiency of the fee system is that it puts pressure on government officials to make sure they are spending fee (tax) revenue wisely and delivering services that will be used.

No matter how a country structures its tax system, it inevitably offers tax credits to reward those who spend money, in pursuit of a

---

7   Binit Das and Arvind Poswal, "Union Budget 2024–25: Why India's Rooftop Solar Plan Fails to Spark Interest," Down to Earth, accessed June 8, 2024, https://www.downtoearth.org.in/renewable-energy/union-budget-2024-25-why-india-s-rooftop-solar-plan-fails-to-spark-interest-94214.

government objective, whether it is childcare, energy production, or new military technology. What may be surprising is how little of the total government budget goes toward the promotion of these goals. As we will show in upcoming chapters, tax credits are not well utilized. In the United States, when the federal government spends $100, only $75 to $80 of that total comes from taxpayers and goes out toward budget categories such as salaries, infrastructure, defense, and military veterans' benefits. The remaining money comes from selling treasury bonds and other American debt obligations; fresh debt is added every year through deficit spending. The process in which the bureaucracy reports its spending needs each year, and the wrangling over budget authorizations and appropriations, is opaque to the average taxpayer. I will present a better system in chapter 6 in which more extensive tax credits would allow the people to dole out money to projects they wanted to support.

THE WHAT AND THE WHY

If you were setting up a natural foods store, *what* you decided to sell would be highly consequential to your success. You could give your vendor a list of *what* you have in mind—the organic vegetables, plant-based milks, and so on. You might also list the sugary, processed foods you don't want to sell. Or you could tell the vendor, "We want to promote the culture of healthy eating." Stating your purpose, the rationale behind the list, puts the *why* at the core of the conversation with the vendor. An understanding develops, making it more likely that over the long run, you will get what you want. **Communicating the *why* is a crucial step in directing tax revenue.** But throughout the world, tax regulations are made public with no background on their value to society—people see what is required, not why. When we encounter a gray area or some unclear text in the regulations affecting our clients, we dig into a document called a budget memorandum that discusses the rationale behind the regulation. That these memoranda are seen only by those who know how to find them, contributes to the public's lack of awareness of the purpose of taxes.

Changing the Mindset on Taxes

Allowing taxpayers to earn a deduction by contributing to a charity or nonprofit is a small concession compared with the shift in mindset that needs to occur. If people feel they are working together with government to build a better society, connecting to a larger purpose, then we will see real, dramatic change. **In any populous democracy, politicians use the tax system to gain access to the hearts of the voting population rather than promoting nation building.** Taxation may be portrayed as a commitment toward nation building, but people can sense how much revenue is deployed to further the interests of those in power. People might not be able to say what percentage of revenue goes where exactly, but **they know for sure that they have no control over government spending, and they lack clarity on why they are paying so much in taxes.**

> To change the mindset on taxes, government must provide a granular accounting of what it wants to spend on and then focus on communicating the *why*.

To change the mindset on taxes, government must provide a granular accounting of what it wants to spend on and then focus on communicating the *why*. It must allow people to earn more tax credits by targeting their payments toward whatever they have a passion for or feel a patriotic need to address. The entire exercise of tax collection could be far happier.

Controlling where our tax payments go should resonate among those of us who run our own businesses, because we got into this position expecting to enjoy feeling in control of all aspects of our entrepreneurial journey. Even when we endure long work hours and business setbacks, we still have the satisfaction of knowing that we don't have to ask a boss for personal time off or permission to spend some money on a project. A less obvious benefit, according to James Clear, author of the best-selling book *Atomic Habits*, is that entrepreneurs live longer, healthier lives than employees do.[8] He cited a study in the *Journal of Occupational and Organizational Psychology* that examined health indicators among a nationally representative sample of German employees and entrepreneurs. The researchers found that entrepreneurs had a significantly lower incidence of physical and mental illnesses, lower blood pressure, lower rates of hypertension, made fewer visits to the hospital, and enjoyed higher overall well-being and life satisfaction. The findings support the theory

> Controlling where our tax payments go should resonate among those of us who run our own businesses, because we got into this position expecting to enjoy feeling in control of all aspects of our entrepreneurial journey.

---

8   James Clear, "Why Everyone Should Act Like an Entrepreneur," (author's website blog entry), accessed August 11, 2023, https://jamesclear.com/health-benefits-entrepreneurship.

that **having higher job demands but more control over your work is less stressful than having lower job demands and less control.**[9]

Transforming the Burden

The proverb that **"nothing in our world is certain but death and taxes"** reflects the common understanding that paying taxes is an inevitable burden. This chapter has outlined a vision for transforming the burden into a challenge, to use this revenue to build a better society. All governments take a share of the value created by their people, and in the process of allocating these resources, they take away a corresponding amount of decision-making authority. Giving some of that authority back to the people is possible but requires more transparency and better communication than we are used to from the bureaucracy. Allowing people to target their taxes toward needs that resonate with them would be a healthy change for society because of the human need to feel in control. This concept of tax alignment, if adopted broadly, could change the world. It may sound far-fetched, but it represents how taxation was supposed to work. History is full of examples of societies built on this principle, as we will see in the next chapter.

> Allowing people to target their taxes toward needs that resonate with them would be a healthy change for society because of the human need to feel in control.

---

9   Ute Stephan and Ulrike Roesler, "Health of Entrepreneurs versus Employees in a National Representative Sample," *Journal of Occupational and Organizational Psychology* 83, no. 3 (December 24, 2010): 717–738, https://doi.org/10.1348/096317909X472067.

CHAPTER 3

Looking Backward–*Putting the Purposes of Tax in Historical Context*

> *TAXES ONCE PROTECTED TRADE,*
> *THEN PRICED ACCESS TO IT–TODAY,*
> *THEY UNLOCK POSSIBILITY.*

Alexander the Great is renowned as one of history's greatest generals, it took not only military prowess, but also money to assemble armies to overthrow the Persian Empire, and embark on conquests as far from Macedonia as India. Consider Alexander's accomplishments at collecting taxes. As he swept around the Mediterranean to Egypt and across the Middle East, a prime task was setting up treasury establishments to fund the military expeditions. In those days, tax was collected in cash, wherever there was hard metal currency, or in kind, as a share of agricultural produce, or through unpaid work, which could include military service. Naturally, a foreign conqueror's levies and conscription provoke hostility, so Alexander and his tax collectors resorted to terror tactics, including executions, to enforce their decrees. It was an impressive display of economic stimulation through plundering, but it was far from groundbreaking. Systematically, recorded taxation dates from at least 5,000 years ago to the Egyptian pharaohs.

Three centuries after Alexander's death, the birth of Jesus happened in Bethlehem—a location required because of taxes. Joseph and Mary, who was pregnant with Jesus, traveled there from Nazareth in time to be enrolled for a tax levied by Caesar Augustus. The founder of the Roman Empire also presided over tax reforms to make property tax levies more systematic and begin introducing the concept of tax collectors as salaried civil servants. Taxes still are sometimes character-ized as a rendering to Caesar, but the concept of taxes as burdensome is even more ancient, as is tax evasion. Archaeologists have discov-ered evidence that wealthy men in ancient Egypt and Mesopotamia hired substitutes or sent slaves to fulfill their obligation to perform work or military service as a payment to the government.[10] Hostility over complicated, regressive, or unfair taxation played a role in many historic uprisings; including the Peasants' Revolt in England in 1381, and the French and American revolutions. Early in American history, a whiskey tax promoted by Alexander Hamilton stirred mob violence and prompted President George Washington to send a well-armed militia to put down the rebellion, helping establish federal power. In 1930, Mohandas (Mahatma) Gandhi kicked off his civil disobedience campaign against British rule in India with a tax protest. He and his followers marched for 21 days from his ashram to the coastal town of Dandi. The Dandi March protested British laws that forced the people to buy heavily taxed salt.

---

10   Joshua J. Mark, "Daily Life in Ancient Mesopotamia," *World History Ency-clopedia*, April 15, 2014, https://www.worldhistory.org/article/680/daily-life-in-ancient-mesopotamia/.

Three Purposes of Tax

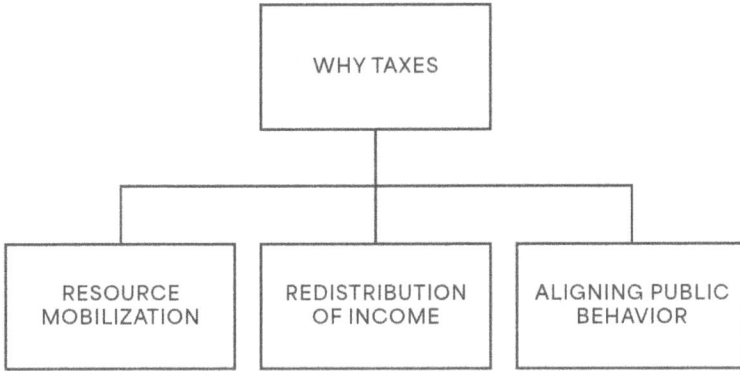

```
                    ┌─────────────────┐
                    │   WHY TAXES     │
                    └────────┬────────┘
          ┌──────────────────┼──────────────────┐
┌─────────┴─────────┐ ┌──────┴──────────┐ ┌──────┴──────────┐
│    RESOURCE       │ │ REDISTRIBUTION  │ │ ALIGNING PUBLIC │
│  MOBILIZATION     │ │   OF INCOME     │ │    BEHAVIOR     │
└───────────────────┘ └─────────────────┘ └─────────────────┘
```

Taxation has both supported and undermined all kinds of needs, causes, and powers throughout history while fulfilling three main purposes: **mobilizing resources, redistributing wealth, and aligning public behavior.** We will see how the first two purposes are inevitable in society and how the third purpose has unexploited potential.

MOBILIZING RESOURCES

The concept of tax emerged in ancient times as humans lived in tribes and contributed toward their common well-being and protection. Tribes expanded into nations over time, and those leading the expansions, whether through greed or ambition, pushed for increasing contributions. They used or abused their power to mobilize resources—appointing tax collectors to give them the wherewithal to establish a dominion. Feudal lords, royal courts, empires, and religions all needed tools to mandate the turnover of labor, agricultural production, and eventually money from their vassals, subjects, and followers.

Taxes were enshrined in law or, in the case of religions, scriptures. The Quran commands Muslims to share their wealth with the payment of Zakat, which traditionally was mandatory but has evolved into individual charitable contributions. Christianity has a tradition of Tithing, where about 10% of income is expected to be contributed to the Church for upkeep of the community. In the case of Hinduism, the law of dharma (moral code) made it mandatory for the haves to take care of the elderly, weak, and needy (without limits). For nations, taxes evolved as political tools, funding a bureaucracy and common public expenses, such as defense. Military conscription, with the possibility of dying for your country, is rooted in the ancient concept of tax as providing service for the protection of the tribe. Historically, and still today, a lot of public funds go into the military. **The United States notably devotes the largest portion of its discretionary budget to military spending at more than $800 billion a year, far more than any other country and more than the next 10 highest-spending countries combined.**[11]

REDISTRIBUTING INCOME

The methods and extent of redistribution are contentious, but all governments engage in some social spending to ensure their stability and public safety. Whenever a government subsidizes healthcare and access to basic amenities for the needy, it is redistributing wealth. **A mechanism for redistribution can be built into direct tax systems through progressive rates, meaning people with higher taxable income pay at a correspondingly higher rate.** Some people characterize redistribution as robbing the rich to pay the poor, and they

---

11   Peter G. Peterson Foundation, chart based on Stockholm International Peace Research Institute Military Expenditure Database, accessed August 15, 2023, https://www.pgpf.org/sites/default/files/0053_defense-comparison.pdf.

argue convincingly that this largesse institutionalizes poverty. In other words, people who believe the government will take care of them lack motivation to lift themselves up. But social spending also improves the business climate by making the streets cleaner and safer, and a better economy creates more revenue. India subsidizes meals for the poor, which in turn leaves them money for shelter, preventing homelessness. The US government provides an eye-popping figure on this use of public funds. It spent more than $1 trillion on benefits and services for people with low income in fiscal 2020 because healthcare costs rose sharply, especially after the COVID-19 pandemic.[12]

ALIGNING PUBLIC BEHAVIOR

Sometimes a government pushes its population to behave in a certain way. Using the tax system for this purpose is not inevitable, in the same way we understand that any government will inevitably raise and spend revenue to maintain the peace and protect against mortal threats such as fires and pandemics. Methods for aligning public behavior are always negotiable. **When the government offers a tax break to push people to be healthier, save more for retirement, resettle in certain places, or work in certain fields, it is an incentive, not a mandate.** To use an ancient example, Muslim rulers imposed a tax called Jizya on their non-Muslim subjects. The motivation was less about the revenue and more about ensuring that people in conquered lands converted to Islam and thereby joined the army. Those who did not want to convert to Islam had to either pay the Jizya or win exemption through the military service of their family members. This classic case of alignment benefited the conquerers because their armies

---

12 Congressional Research Service, Federal Spending on Benefits and Services for People with Low Income: FY2008-FY2020, R46986, December 8, 2021, https://crsreports.congress.gov/product/pdf/R/R46986.

were significantly outnumbered by the native religious practitioners in their new territories.

Three Ps of Tax Alignment

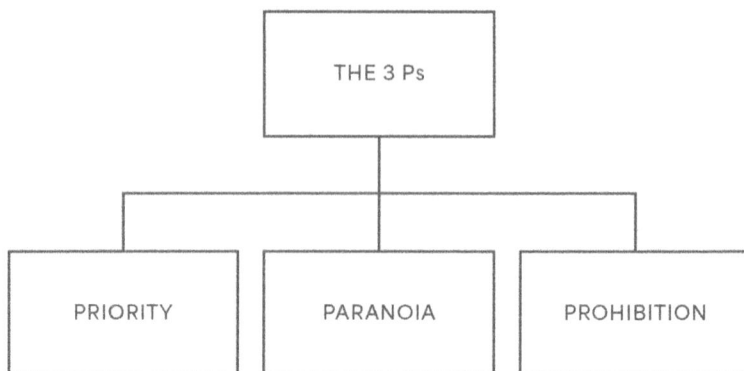

```
        ┌─────────────────┐
        │                 │
        │     THE 3 Ps    │
        │                 │
        └────────┬────────┘
                 │
    ┌────────────┼────────────┐
    │            │            │
┌───────────┐ ┌──────────┐ ┌─────────────┐
│           │ │          │ │             │
│ PRIORITY  │ │ PARANOIA │ │ PROHIBITION │
│           │ │          │ │             │
└───────────┘ └──────────┘ └─────────────┘
```

Historically, across jurisdictions, systems of tax collection and incentives have three broad categories of policies for the alignment of public behavior. We can call these the three Ps because they stem from the government's **Priorities, Paranoia, and Prohibitions.**

Priorities are activities that governments want their people and businesses to engage in, including both short- and long-term incentives. Governments have an ongoing interest in keeping their citizens employed and paying taxes, so they typically give entrepreneurs job-creation credits. In a highly populous country like India, generating employment is high on the government's agenda, so a company supplying jobs will be rewarded. Not only are the wages paid considered business expenses; those hiring more than 10 people get a generous additional tax break. Other incentives target specific sectors. In a country like the United States, which is trying to decrease its dependence on certain imports from certain countries, a business offering to manufacture those products domestically will get tax credits.

Promotion of tourism is a priority in countries as diverse as Serbia, Singapore, and Switzerland, all of which have turned to indirect tax credits to lure foreign film producers. The Hindi-language romantic movie *Dilwale Dulhania Le Jayenge* (*The Big-Hearted Will Take the Bride*) has now been playing in India's theaters for over 30 years. It was shot in part in Switzerland, which consequently became a hot tourist destination soon after for wealthy Indians, so much so that Swiss railroads have named trains after the director of that film and other Bollywood figures.[13] That tourism marketing is a classic case of joint public-private alignment to encourage economic activity. If you go to Mount Titlis, a popular day trip from Lucerne, you can see the film promoted with a poster made of life-size cutouts and snack on Indian samosas and drink chai in the snowy Swiss Alps.

> That tourism marketing is a classic case of joint public-private alignment to encourage economic activity.

Paranoia refers to assets or capabilities that the government considers strategic or extremely valuable and doesn't want to lose. Perhaps the best example of this is the global crisis in the semiconductor industry in the early 2020s. East Asia has dominated this space, and tax incentives for these companies are among the highest globally. During that crisis, China gave a 100% subsidy on

---

13   Anand Chandrasekhar, "On the Trail of the First Indian Film Shot in Switzerland," SWI swissinfo.ch, January 28, 2024, https://www.swissinfo.ch/eng/culture/55-years-later_on-the-trail-of-the-first-indian-film-shot-in-switzerland/45016464; Anand Chandrasekhar, "Swiss Honour Indian Filmmaker Yash Chopra with Statue," SWI swissinfo.ch, January 28, 2024, https://www.swissinfo.ch/eng/culture/tourism-ambassador_swiss-honour-indian-filmmaker-yash-chopra-with-statue/42128072.

land for companies that start semiconductor businesses. China also offered a 75% rebate on corporate taxes. The United States was not far behind, offering a 50% tax subsidy on land acquisitions during that period. The higher the level of paranoia, such as when national security is threatened, the more likely it is that the tax breaks become so enormous that they seem borderline insane.

> The higher the level of paranoia, such as when national security is threatened, the more likely it is that the tax breaks become so enormous that they seem borderline insane.

When we look at countries that are net importers, primarily because they lack energy resources or the capacity to manufacture goods, foreign currency reserves become a strategic asset. In Malaysia, the government provides 10% to 100% tax incentives for companies exporting in designated sectors. In India, the government gives a certain share of gross exports as cash back to companies earning in foreign exchange. Paranoia is not too strong a word to describe how a government reacts to the destabilizing prospect of having insufficient foreign currency to meet its obligations. Tax incentives encouraging domestic manufacturing of needed goods can reduce the outflow of foreign currency for imports. Paranoia about the extent of oil imports was behind India's incentives to invest in solar, hydro, and wind energy, and today India is one of the largest producers of renewable energy.

Here's how a successful green energy program worked in India: wind energy companies, instead of raising capital to build windmills, were allowed to sell windmills to wealthy individuals who had no other connection to that industry. Normally such a large commercial-equipment purchase would be written off on taxes over the years based on a depreciation schedule. But the individual's entire investment was allowed as a tax reduction in the first year because the government wanted more windmills. Both the energy companies and the investors received incentives, but the accelerated depreciation jump-started the program. Similar schemes around the world exist wherever **governments focus tax incentives on sectors they deem critical.**

Prohibition refers to activities that, for various reasons, the government doesn't want to encourage—at least not publicly. Typically, these are "sin goods" such as tobacco, alcohol, and cannabis. Businesses in this space can expect to be taxed consistently and heavily wherever they operate. Prohibitions have always endured very high taxes and importance because governments have always depended on vices to augment resources. Pope Leo X was notorious for levying taxes on licensed prostitution. The advantage of putting up with high taxes for these ever-reliable businesses is that governments grow dependent on the revenue and thereby supply indirect patronage. In my home state of Tamil Nadu, the state-owned liquor distributor is the largest and most profitable retailer in all of India. So, even though the government controls liquor sales to regulate its use, it also has a state interest in promoting its sale.

The classic American example involves gambling and the historic government efforts to limit exceptions to its prohibition to certain places such as Las Vegas. Limiting the supply of casinos in the face of strong demand ensured the growth of profitable businesses whose revenue could be taxed because it was not hidden underground. Legalized cannabis has followed the same course as gambling, alcohol, and tobacco, to become highly regulated and taxed industries. The government advocates restraint on moral, ethical, or health grounds, but it also provides protection. Investments in these industries have generated hundreds of billions of dollars of wealth over the years because of the way governments are aligning public behavior.

Consumers spend at government-sanctioned businesses, which collect a hefty consumption tax that comes from the pockets of those buying something to drink or smoke.

Despite the posturing, especially around election times, about the dangers of protecting "sin goods," governments have no interest in shutting down profitable industries such as cigarette companies any more than they are going to shut down the oil companies that fuel the economy and generate gasoline taxes. Such industries may pay lawsuit settlements, endure more regulation than other businesses, and lose out on some ESG investing from those who adhere to environmental, social, and governance standards. But we hardly see tobacco, liquor, or oil companies going bankrupt. **The prohibition category of policy involves a constant trade-off between conscience and collections.**

Why This Matters

Understanding the purposes of taxation and how it evolved helps us see why governments around the world structure policies to meet their own needs and desires. Then we can **devise strategies to take control of our taxes rather than be controlled by the tax systems and regulations.** Use of taxation to mobilize resources and redistribute wealth have proven to be necessary levers for a successful economy and society. They are contentious because they promote inefficiency in the system, but they provide much-needed security, safety, or predictability to our lives and our busi-

> Understanding the purposes of taxation and how it evolved helps us see why governments around the world structure policies to meet their own needs and desires.

nesses. The less-inevitable purpose of taxation is to push people to behave in a certain way, to align with the government's agenda.

With this historical foundation and understanding of alignment's facets in place, we're ready to explore practical applications. While these strategies can benefit individuals and society at large, we begin by examining how businesses can harness the power of tax alignment to ultimately see tax as a possibility as opposed to an eventuality.

PART II

Integration

CHAPTER 4

Attention Entrepreneurs— *Devising a Strategy of Tax Alignment for Your Business*

> *TAX IS NOT "WHAT YOU PAY,"*
>
> *IT'S "WHAT YOU ENDURE"*

Our client Mark called to ask for help analyzing how best to outsource some software development. Mark knew from experience that developers in India could do the work for less money than anyone he could hire in San Francisco, where his company was located. But he had heard the Philippines and Vietnam were also competing for his kind of offshoring business.

"Which place would be the cheapest in terms of setting this up?" Mark asked.

I replied that we needed to flip the question around and ask, "Where can you earn the most?"

Mark had not heard anyone put it that way before, and he was intrigued, so we went ahead and set up a competitive chart that would factor in tax incentives and other concessions. Mark's business was selling software to companies in the FMCG (fast-moving consumer goods) industry. Maximizing his profits involved a lot more than Mark simply offshoring the software development to the place with the cheapest labor and office space. He needed certain qualities in the workforce, which ruled out Vietnam, at that time. The Philippines had the edge on cost, but let's examine why Mark ended up importing his software from Bangalore, in India, and not Manila.

I explained that Mark needed to pay attention to aligning his business interests with the host country's governmental priorities and paranoia, two of the three Ps we discussed in the previous chapter. The government of India would reward him for creating jobs there, a national priority, and bringing in foreign currency, which is a matter of paranoia for almost all net-importing countries. Bangalore offered Mark a tax break that amounted to a 30% rebate on the employee cost, which already was almost half of what he would pay in the West. For every $100 in salaries his software subsidiary company registered in India paid to its developers, the government allowed a deduction of $130. By having the development company establish its office in a special economic zone, that cost was also heavily subsidized. Import duties were waived on hundreds of thousands of dollars of high-end servers and other technical infrastructure brought in for the office because the software company's products would all be exported from India to Mark's US-based sales company. As an added incentive, the government offered about 2% to 5% of the gross value of exports as cash back and waived any income tax on the company's profits for 10 years.

This flood of rewards remains memorable to me over 10 years later, but substantial tax incentives exist in most parts of the world. To find these rewards, entrepreneurs must broaden their vision and learn **how much they can earn, rather than focus on what they might spend.**

This strategy works for companies of all sizes in various industries. It doesn't matter if you make semiconductors or bicycles. It doesn't matter if your company is international or domestic, or has less than $1 million or more than $1 billion in revenue. It's simply a matter of shifting your mindset from viewing taxes as a hardship you must bear to realizing that taxes can be used to your advantage if you align your interests with the government.

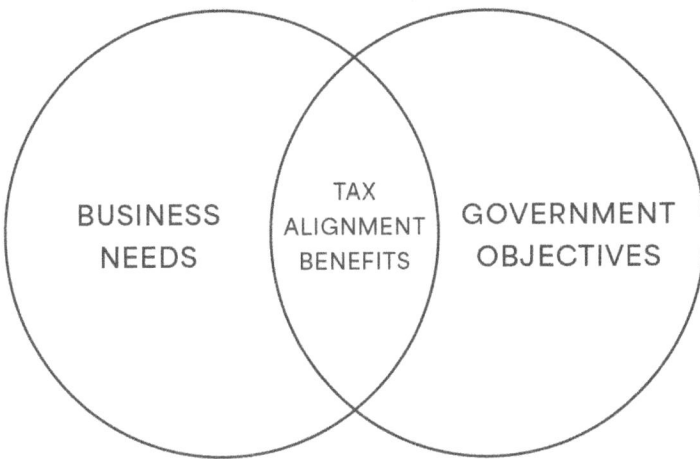

A Huge Gray Area

Data on how much it costs to do business in a jurisdiction is relatively easy to find, compared with the difficulty of determining how tax incentives may affect the eventual bottom line. We will discuss more in part III of this book on how to overcome the barriers to accessing and being certain of the effects of tax alignment. For now, let's focus on the fact that tax incentives are out there somewhere for those who know how to look for them through the bureaucratic haze and integrate them into their business strategy. They go by many names, and the regulations and rewards vary widely, depending on the jurisdiction. The clearest way to see the variation is to look at data available for developed nations. The Center for Strategic and International Studies (CSIS), a private, nonpartisan institution focusing on international public policy issues, analyzed how much various countries spend on subsidies and tax credits. Back in 2019, before the COVID-19 pandemic and geopolitics changed the landscape, the US government spent less than its key allies and its top economic competitor, China, on subsidies and tax credits. With respect to gross domestic product, the United States spent about 0.4% of its GDP on tax incentives, R&D support, direct subsidies, and below-market credit, an abysmally low amount for a developed country. China was spending almost 1.5%, nearly four times the United States. The Americans had some catching up to do, which helped lead to the Infrastructure Investment and Jobs Act of 2021, which allocated $1.2 trillion, most notably for addressing climate change through energy policy and transportation programs.[14]

Tax credits, tax holidays, capital subsidies, and investment subsidies are some of the forms that incentives can take. If the US government wants to encourage domestic production of semiconductors, for instance, it can give one or more manufacturers tax credits to offset production costs, delay taxing sales revenue, or subsidize investments to acquire land and build and equip a plant. However, a government's many levels of jurisdiction, departments,

---

14 "H.R.3684—Infrastructure Investment and Jobs Act," US Government Publishing Office, November 15, 2021, https://www.congress.gov/bill/117th-congress/house-bill/3684/text.

and agencies rarely, if ever, work together on these incentives. It's the bureaucratic version of the left hand not knowing what the right hand is doing.

Making Government Work for You

For entrepreneurs, the route to profit from tax is to position their business in accordance with the regulations. For Mark, that meant devoting extra effort to complying with regulations and placing his business in a special economic zone, which turned out to be a great location. Entrepreneurs often assume incorrectly that tax incentives come with a lot of strings attached that would force them to act against their instincts or best interests. Our experience instead has been that incentives help entrepreneurs structure their businesses better. **The reason for this is that incentives exist because someone has made a case that they would have some impact.** The incentives signal to the entrepreneur that the government has seen market potential in their industry and is working to increase that market. **Aligning yourself with the governmental incentives helps you clarify your own product market fit.** For Mark, that meant the government was investing in making Bangalore the Silicon Valley of

> Aligning yourself with the governmental incentives helps you clarify your own product market fit.

India, so he would find the workforce and resources there to be a good fit. When the government offered him and others generous rewards, it took on the onus of promoting development of the region that benefited participants in the incentive programs by building momentum in the local tech sector.

The structure of the global economy, in which the US dollar is an international reserve currency, is an important component of making governments work for businesses. Readers familiar with the history of the dollar and with the fact that delegates from 44 nations met in Bretton Woods, New Hampshire, to establish an international monetary system in 1944 won't need the basic background information that follows in this paragraph. **Every country that is a net importer of goods or services from abroad, including the United States, needs dollars to cover its trade—a major source of government paranoia.** For example, when an oil-dependent nation pays Saudi Arabia in dollars, it must generate foreign currency to pay for the import. Promoting an industry that can export services, as the software developers were doing in Bangalore, restores the foreign exchange reserves as the company exchanges its dollars for rupees to pay its employees and bills. **Foreign currency reserves are critical to ensure the sustenance of any government with a negative balance of trade, which includes most of the world's developing countries.** If they run short of dollars, they must pay a premium, which can lead to debt, currency devaluation, inflation, and other economic challenges.

The beauty of the tax-alignment strategy for businesses is that it doesn't matter how big or small they are, or what industry they are in. If your industry is oil or agriculture, you already know certain areas are more likely than others to have tax incentives set up for your market. And you may have places in mind where you are more comfortable operating. With just those two criteria, you can narrow your search, like people do when they are relocating their family for better schools or settling on a retirement-friendly area. They start off thinking about their needs, and the more thorough the research they do, the more likely they will be to land in a place where the government has crafted favorable tax regulations. Some entrepreneurs will search the whole world, and others will focus on a small area, but they should be asking the same questions: "What benefits are available for what I intend to do? What districts desperately want to attract this activity?" **Entrepreneurs know how to market themselves to customers and clients eager for their products and services, but they often fail to target tax jurisdictions that are desperately needing what they are creating.**

> Some entrepreneurs will search the whole world, and others will focus on a small area, but they should be asking the same questions: "What benefits are available for what I intend to do? What districts desperately want to attract this activity?"

WHERE IN THE WORLD WAS THAT CAR MADE?

You may remember the time-traveling car in the *Back to the Future* movies but not be aware that its model, a DeLorean DMC-12, also played a starring role in a tax-incentive drama.[15] The DeLorean Motor Company, founded in 1975 by American John DeLorean, produced only this one model of sports car with gull-wing doors and went bankrupt by 1982. To start his own auto company, the former General Motors executive scouted around the world for locations, desperate for jobs and willing to help pay the costs of establishing a manufacturing

---

15   Business Bliss Consultants FZE, "DeLorean Motor Company: Northern Ireland Conflict," UKDiss.com, accessed November 14, 2023, https://ukdiss.com/examples/delorean-motor-company-northern-ireland-conflict.php.

plant. The British government provided concessions worth at least £77 million (about $100 million) to have the plant built in strife-torn Northern Ireland. DeLorean aligned his business with the priorities of a government that hoped auto plant jobs would promote political stability.[16] Northern Ireland was an unlikely location for car manufacturing, as it was disconnected from supply lines and lacked a workforce of skilled autoworkers. Plenty of other factors shared the blame when DeLorean's venture failed, but it remains a classic case of a business strategy misalignment.

We've Seen That Movie

Certain industries have mastered tax alignment in familiar ways. Film producers shop around the globe for locations that not only fit the script but also offer lavish incentives. Governments seek to promote tourism by showcasing their scenic locations; Dubai was able to show off the world's tallest building, Burj Khalifa, during a Tom Cruise stunt in the fourth *Mission Impossible* film. Many Indian films have been shot in Switzerland, Serbia, Malaysia, and Singapore. At DVS Advisors, we helped a client look for countries with suitable mountain topography that would offer tax breaks for a $20 million film production. Serbia came through, and the client got 25% of its production costs back. Countries also use incentives to make themselves hubs of an industry, as Panama did with shipping. Panama made ship registration convenient and offered a simpler and predictable regulatory

---

16   Gerry Moriarty, "Back to the Failure: Belfast's £77 Million Sports Car," *Irish Times*, November 22, 2014, https://www.irishtimes.com/news/ireland/irish-news/back-to-the-failure-belfast-s-77-million-sports-car-1.2010638.

regime compared to other countries, but it also charged no income tax. Singapore and Dubai subsidized and modernized port infrastructure to become shipping hubs in their regions. In each case, the government expected to benefit from peripheral developments by attracting an industry.

A barrier to alignment occurs when the government decides its interests would be served by a prohibition. Some US states legalized the recreational sale of marijuana, while growing and selling cannabis remained a federal crime. The states planned to get a revenue windfall by taxing an emerging business sector, but the companies had no way to deduct their costs on federal tax forms.[17] The cannabis companies, facing disproportionately high taxes, had to pass the costs along to remain profitable. Many customers were willing to absorb the higher costs. But some businesses failed, some consumers turned to cheaper black market sources, and some localities were forced to lower tax rates—all symptoms of imperfect alignment.

For entrepreneurs who don't have an obvious place to start looking for tax alignment, they might take inspiration from Simon Sinek's best-selling book on leadership *Start with Why*.[18] Using Sinek's perspective on human behavior, you would start with the question "Why are you in this business?" or "Why do you want to start this business?" Let's hope it is your passion and resonates with you. The next questions moving outward in the three concentric rings in Sinek's Golden Circle are "How?" and "What?" As you examine how you are going to implement your business plan and what you might specialize in as your appropriate and profitable niche, you will see what you bring to

---

17 "Cannabis Industry FAQ," US Internal Revenue Service, updated June 6, 2024, https://www.irs.gov/businesses/small-businesses-self-employed/cannabis-industry-frequently-asked-questions.

18 Simon Sinek, *Start with Why* (New York: Portfolio, an imprint of Penguin Random House, 2009).

the table. **The specific thing you can do to make money will lead you to find matching incentives.** The research involved can begin with a simple online search once you have narrowed your focus from your industry to your core activity. Even Apple, often ranked as the world's largest technology company, has a clear focus in its business. It doesn't manufacture iPhones but designs and markets them and oversees the complex supply chain for a limited number of products.

If your business is not a worldwide household name, what is its maximum scope? Some entrepreneurs feel tied to wherever their office is, perhaps because they have supportive friends and family there. In that case, their search for tax alignment will have a narrow scope. If you are restricting your business to one country, are state-level incentives available? If so, what are the top three states? These are the kinds of questions we start with in seeking tax alignment.

Getting Professional Guidance

At DVS Advisors, we have walked clients through this process around the world successfully, and we believe professional guidance is the best way to develop an alignment strategy. **We prepare a matrix to match their needs and resources with various parameters in the tax incentives, such as minimum number of employees, required capital investment, years the incentive is available, and difficulty of compliance.** We offer a score on the bureaucratic engagement expected in each location. Tax incentives require a business to interact substantially with the local bureaucracy, and it can be frustrating if both sides are not up to the job. The ease of movements of funds and foreign currency is another important factor in the matrix.

We also know that the best deal on paper may not work out. The business operators may be uncomfortable dealing with the people, culture, or government there. We include a score for the comfort factor in the matrix because it does not make sense to search for tax alignment in areas where you would be uncomfortable setting up a business. We encourage clients to educate themselves about the local culture as part of the decision to open a business abroad. Some areas have a workforce that's a better fit for some companies' culture. We refer them to books where they can learn beyond stereotypes about the values and ways of the people they would be working with. We were attracted to working in Singapore because it is very business friendly, but a London-based client discovered the hard way that an East Asian site was not a good fit. Culturally, there were challenges on accommodating the time difference to work with the UK head-quarters. The office moved to another country even though it meant paying about 10% more in taxes.

More likely, the journey to derive alignment from where you set up your business will turn out better than expected. **Behind the tax incentive are politicians and a state establishment that created the program and are vested in its success.** They will **work on behalf of the businesses they attracted, to create a supporting ecosystem to yield positive results.** When our clients are looking to set up a business abroad, we research the political climate in their target country and the protection it offers. For example, if you were to invest in Indonesia from Singapore, where they have a bilateral investment protection agreement, that means that come what may, the investments in Indonesia are protected by a sovereign guarantee by the state from any intrusion. Similarly, we look for DTAA networks, which are double tax avoidance agreements. Singapore has the largest such network in the world, and similarly, India has treaties with over 100 countries to avoid double taxation.

PLAYING THE LONG GAME

As Tesla developed into an international manufacturer of electric vehicles over 20 years, it added plants in Canada, Europe, and China alongside its original factory in California. Discussions began with India in 2021, and Tesla CEO Elon Musk met with Indian Prime Minister Narendra Modi in the United States in June 2023. Yet hopes among some people that Tesla would soon announce a plant in India went unfulfilled. Details of Tesla's talks with Indian officials are not public, but it's no secret that tax incentives have played a big role in the ups and downs of Tesla's fortunes. For example, when Tesla rolled out a moderately priced midsize sedan in 2017, buyers benefited from a US federal tax credit of up to $7,500. India offered a huge consumer market for Tesla if it could win that kind of favorable treatment, while the American company's manufacturing presence would produce jobs and clean-energy benefits for India. But alignment is not that simple in such a dynamic global industry in which India may want to compete not only with Tesla, but also manufacturers in China and South Korea. India could bide its time in talks with Tesla because it was extracting foreign currency from the electric car boom. India's then commerce minister, Piyush Goyal, said publicly that Tesla bought $1 billion of auto components from India in 2022, and that figure was expected to nearly double in 2023.[19] In 2024, it appeared possible that Tesla would soon begin building showrooms and service centers to sell EVs in

---

19   Jagmeet Singh, "Tesla Plans to Almost Double Component Sourcing from India to $1.9B This Year, Says Minister," *Techcrunch*, September 13, 2023, https://techcrunch.com/2023/09/13/tesla-india-component-sourcing.

India after the government committed to slashing the import duties for five years for manufacturers willing to invest US$500 million for their EV projects.[20] The first of those showrooms has since opened.

A Winning Strategy

Some companies view the entire world as their playing field, but most need to make smart choices about where they will do business. Instead of focusing on where it is cheapest, they should consider how the government's priorities and paranoia have led to incentives that turn tax into profit. With professional help, they can evaluate legal, bureaucratic, cultural, and other factors to decide where they can make governments work for them. This strategy, available to all kinds of businesses, rewards those who participate, and it can take on additional momentum when an area's tax incentives create a supportive ecosystem.

> Instead of focusing on where it is cheapest, they should consider how the government's priorities and paranoia have led to incentives that turn tax into profit.

---

20   Murali Gopalan, "For Tesla, India Can Perhaps Wait for Now," *Economic Times*, April 27, 2024, https://auto.economictimes.indiatimes.com/news/passenger-vehicle/for-tesla-india-can-perhaps-wait-for-now/109638467.

Takeaways for Entrepreneurs

- Substantial tax incentives exist in most parts of the world for businesses that align their interests with those of a host country.
- **Focus on how much you can earn given the available rewards, not just on comparing the costs of doing business. Tax is the cost for nonalignment.**
- **When national priorities become business goals, taxes become incentives.**
- **The alignment approach** works irrespective of your size, industry, or geography—all it takes is a Mindset of Possibility.
- Start looking for incentives in the places familiar to you and your industry, but don't assume there aren't other, better places you might find with professional guidance.

DISCOVER MILLION DOLLAR INCENTIVES YOU DIDN'T KNOW YOU COULD CLAIM

Scan the QR code below to access our *Global Incentive Finder*—a powerful tool to uncover the best tax incentives available for your business, anywhere in the world.

CHAPTER 5

Going All In—How Policymakers Can Use Tax Alignment for Society's Benefit

WHOM YOU ATTRACT MATTERS MORE THAN HOW MUCH YOU COLLECT.

Everyone who drives a car knows we pay one way or another for the roads that get us where we are going. Depending on where we live, a road tax may have been integrated into the price of our car, fuel, or annual vehicle registration, combined with user fees that include tolls based on distance traveled, bridges and tunnels traversed, and truck weights. **The funding systems and spending decisions can be contentious when people feel their needs are being neglected or are paying more than their fair share.** The US federal, state, and local governments all spend significant amounts of their general revenue building and maintaining roads, to the consternation of those taxpayers who don't own cars and rarely venture far from home. Then there is the system in Dubai, where every drive on Sheikh Zayed Road and some of the other major thoroughfares is charged electronically to the car owner.

Since 2007, Dubai has required all vehicles to have stickers called Salik tags that are readable electronically at toll gates, including those on Sheikh Zayed Road, which is the busiest corridor in the city-state and connects the seven United Arab Emirates. This toll system is a brilliant example of alignment, and I make that argument as someone who has lived in Dubai, works in Dubai, and sees the tolls show up on my mobile phone bill. Driving on the wide, high-speed Sheikh Zayed Road is expensive but convenient, as there are free alternate routes that help limit traffic. But at some point, every car must travel on the toll roads because they are indispensable to getting around the UAE. The users don't mind paying, for two reasons. First, the alternative would be taxes that drive up the costs of either their cars or fuel. And second, the high-tech collection mechanism is frictionless, with the charge automatically showing up on a monthly bill. Salik originated as a government project, and it proved so profitable that in 2022, the government took it public. The government remains the majority shareholder, but allows investors to buy shares. In other words, it is possible to drive on world-class roads and earn a dividend from their existence. Meanwhile, development flourished on both sides of the Sheikh Zayed Road, improving Dubai's entire economy. Using toll collections to build better infrastructure is an example of tax alignment for your community.

User fees give people a sense of control over how the government is spending their money. Psychologically, it is human nature to enjoy giving—when we do it by choice rather than by requirement. This feeling of control is like the lure that led to the rise of discount airfares that give consumers a choice of whether to pay separately for checked luggage, seat selection, blankets, meals, and tiny bottles of wine and liquor. **The low-cost, no-frills airlines are among the most profitable because a lot of people are willing to pay for the extras when it's their choice to do so.** Also, these airlines are not wasting time or money delivering services people don't value enough to pay for. Similarly, when a government relies on fees to develop infrastructure or provide services, it learns through experience to deliver improvements that make people more willing to use the facilities or services. The outcome is a virtuous cycle of increased consumption resulting in increased collection and more revenue to fund further improvements. The promise of better roads or other public resources is an incentive, and human beings always respond to incentives. It's the best way for governments to align a certain kind of public behavior at sufficient scale to make a difference in society.

> When a government relies on fees to develop infrastructure or provide services, it learns through experience to deliver improvements that make people more willing to use the facilities or services.

Overcoming Distrust

Let's consider a hypothetical case in which a developing country has a lot of vacant land in its cities, a small investor class, and a restless young population with a high unemployment rate. The government announces subsidies for investors who commit to building a football stadium in any city of a certain population size. The stadiums are intended to create jobs in construction, maintenance, travel, lodging, and food services that would receive related tax incentives. Eventually, the government expects to get a revenue windfall from the development. **But that plan doesn't stand a chance of fulfilling its potential if the government's focus on tax enforcement and collection is much more vigorous than its implementation of the subsidy and incentive programs.** The tax collectors have short-term revenue targets to fulfill, which they must meet one way or another. Investors have little basis to trust that their stadium-related tax breaks will not be denied on some technicality. They may ask for clarity and get noncommittal answers from the tax office because the program is new and untested. We will dive deeper into detail in Chapter 8 about how governments can offer tax credits tied to specific projects that are publicized in a way that citizens can be sure they are approved to move forward. For now, let's discuss why such tax credits are a good idea.

Suppose the government has determined it is a priority to build a football stadium or address some other community need, such as a new school or library. Funding may come from a complex mix of sources, including federal, state, and local taxes, private enterprise, and foundation grants. These sources could all be described as indirect funding. People paid their taxes because they had to, they invested in the private enterprise to make money, and they donated to the foundation to support its general mission. They were not voting with their wallets for that stadium, school, or library. **If the local government took direct contributions from taxpayers for those projects in exchange for tax credits, it would give the citizens control over how their taxes are being spent. That element of control, including seeing the manifestation of their contribution, would automatically eradicate the feeling that taxes are a burden.**

Of course, not all taxes can be linked to projects that citizens fund directly, because the government has many spending needs that are obligatory or too arcane to explain to the general population. Governments can use consumption taxes to fund noncontribution expenses such as bureaucratic salaries and the military. But even if only a quarter of expenditures were funded by these contributions linked to tax credits, **people would welcome the idea of allocating their money to something that helps their communities advance and prosper. This approach of voluntary contributions could gradually expand to eventually replace income tax.**

A Vision for More Popular Choice

Bureaucrats put out a list of bridges that need repair or replacement, for example, and allow people to decide which ones they want to pay for with a contribution credited as a tax payment. By choosing a cause that resonates with them, the people would enjoy more control and be more satisfied with government. Those passionate about care for elderly people or better parks could put their money there. People in the military could put their money toward the programs that serve veterans. Of course, the government still would budget to fulfill its fixed obligations and fund necessary programs that might be too arcane to attract public support. But **giving taxpayers discretionary control over even a fraction of the government's budget would leave them less at a loss as to how their money was spent.** It would make them stakeholders in the system and provide more accountability and transparency in government spending than we have now.

Suppose a government currently allows taxpayers to donate $1,000 to the charities of their choice and get some deduction or credit in return. The charities are required to be transparent about where the money goes, and the onus is on the donors to learn to their satisfaction whether the money is being well spent. A similar system of government accountability would start by making spending requests transparent, with bureaucrats reporting them up the chain to their superiors. Governments sometimes put certain spending up for a referendum, but that is simply an up or down vote on a bond levy, rate increase, or construction project that has already worked its way up the chain. A system in which tax credits were more extensive would not replace the political processes in which final budget decisions are made, but it would give people more of a voice at the beginning of those processes. Letting the people designate even 10% or 20% of the budget could pay for itself by discouraging tax evasion, which is pervasive across societies.

> Letting the people designate even 10% or 20% of the budget could pay for itself by discouraging tax evasion, which is pervasive across societies.

Recent advances in behavioral economics make it possible for us to create a system that people can understand and use efficiently to direct their tax money. Richard Thaler, a professor at the University of Chicago Booth School of Business, used research in psychology to explore an alternative to heavy-handed government regulation. He made the case that governments could make policies that nudge citizens to make better choices, rather than making compliance compulsory. Thaler coauthored a 2008 bestseller, *Nudge: Improving Decisions About Health, Wealth and Happiness*, and won the 2017 Nobel Memorial Prize in Economic Science. A classic example of a nudge in the American tax system can be seen in the 401(k) program in which the government encourages employees to set aside money for retirement by having the employer move a portion of each paycheck into a tax-deferred account. Participation rises when this kind of savings and investment option is clear, simple, and happens by default. Those who wish to self-direct their contribution can do so, but more passive investors still have money set aside. Someone who turns 65 years old in 2088 may be defaulted into a mutual fund customized to that target date. They know why it is happening, even if they don't know exactly what the specific investments are or how bonds or mutual funds work. This popular option stands in stark contrast to the complexity of the overall US tax system requiring complex forms and calculation to earn most kinds of tax credits.

Savings bond programs provide some precedent for the funding of society's needs through direct voluntary contributions to the government. Any citizen of India, including not just employees, but students, self-employed individuals, and children, can contribute to the Public Provident Fund (PPF). The contribution is tax deductible and can be redeemed tax-free with interest, currently around 7%, after 15 years, extendable in blocks of five years indefinitely. A fast-growing 2015 program encourages parents in India to build a fund for the future education and marriage expenses of their female child by opening an account at a post office or authorized bank.

Building on Existing Resources

Some communities become hubs of a particular industry because of their geography or natural resources. For example, oil and natural gas riches helped make Houston the fourth largest US city. Technology hubs, in contrast, require a mix of resources, such as local universities that are strong in science, mathematics, and engineering; alongside willing investor; and sympathetic regulators. It helps, of course, if they happen to be the home of ingenious inventors like the young men who founded Apple and Google. No matter how a hub develops, the communities would be remiss if they did not try to build on their good fortune. If a city has oil drillers, it should start giving incentives to attract companies that manufacture drilling equipment. If it has a silicon chip–making plant, it should incentivize related businesses to locate nearby. Technology has allowed more people to work from anywhere, but substantial opportunities remain for society to use tax incentives to attract allied businesses, institutions, and digital nomads to promote economic growth.

When governments offer tax credits tied to specific projects, they are expanding or building on the traditional recognition that businesses and individuals should have an incentive to support nonprofit organizations that serve community needs. Governments have enough major unmet priorities that they don't need to impede any tax-collection rules that keep religious and charitable organizations, foundations, and land-preservation trusts from pursuing their missions. *Our premise is that top government spending priorities will seem compelling to a significant proportion of the taxpaying population.* These people will be willing to contribute to those priority projects that resonate with them. Because they will receive tax credits in return, it would be money they already owed to the tax collector, and it would not result in a reduction of their charitable giving.

> Our premise is that top government spending priorities will seem compelling to a significant proportion of the taxpaying population.

We should stipulate that smaller government units will find this type of tax alignment easier to implement. The countries with the largest economies have well-documented issues with budget deficits. They have also evolved complex revenue systems to deal with a wide range of geographic, political, industrial, and commercial interests. A city-state like Dubai is better positioned than a large country to have one regimen for a function such as collecting highway tolls. It's no accident that Americans leave a lot of decisions about funding education infrastructure to the 13,000 or so school districts around the country.[21] Their geography and demographics determine their property tax collection, and the higher it is, the more likely families with school-age children will be attracted to live there. Growing the community's population that is willing and able to pay for good schools creates a virtuous circle for that district.

Attracting Foreign Investment

Lee Kuan Yew, the founding prime minister of modern Singapore credited with building its booming economy, came into office in a city-state with high unemployment, low literacy, and other hobbling legacies of colonial rule. In a 1967 speech, Lee famously compared modern Singapore to what he said it was when Sir Stamford Raffles founded it in 1819: "150 souls in a minor fishing village."[22] Singapore had a port and some manufacturing at independence in 1965, but the small island had no natural resources. Lee's primary focus was to build a society where the systems would be self-funded and people, including foreign investors, would feel free to explore their opportunities. Lee created a stable and orderly political regime—with low taxes—that lured multinational companies and became a global financial center. Along with another former British colony, Hong Kong, Singapore is a role model to the world in how to generate revenue that establishes a budget surplus.

---

21   National Center for Education Statistics, "Table 214.10. Number of Public School Districts and Public and Private Elementary and Secondary Schools: Selected Years, 1869–70 through 2020–21," Digest of Education Statistics, 2022, https://nces.ed.gov/programs/digest/d22/tables/dt22_214.10.asp.

22   "Late Singapore Leader Lee Kuan Yew Had Opinions on Everything," TIME, March 22, 2015, https://time.com/3748654/singapore-lee-kuan-yews-opinions/.

Every society has infrastructure demands, from age-old needs like bridges or water supply distribution and treatment, to cutting-edge technology for airports. Some of it gets approved; some of it gets shot down, often for lack of funds—or lack of imagination about how to attract capital. Foreign investors should not have to argue with the government over whether they are eligible to put money into a community project. Protectionism and national security concerns are the main reasons governments draw up complicated rules for foreign investors. For example, if a coastal city develops a port that is foreign owned, its future is beholden to that external relationship. A more flexible alternative, which we will explore further in Chapter 8, would be a mechanism in which the foreign investors only need to persuade the government to enroll their community project as state funded. Their contributions toward that project become credits for state taxes payable from the proceeds of the enterprise. Even investors not in a position to receive the tax credit still might be attracted by advance assurance that the state has approved the project. **Especially in democracies, government has powerful gatekeepers at all levels, and foreign investors feel a lack of control over how this system operates.** The community, meanwhile, has assurance that accountability for the project rests with the state.

Fulfilling a Leader's Vision

A strategy of tax alignment to benefit society is hardly a new idea. More than 1,000 years ago in southern India's Chola dynasty, when kings conquered a territory, they sent out a surveyor to decide which lands could be cultivated. The kings then gave these fertile lands to the Brahmins to distribute to the Vellala, the farmer caste, and to society's service providers who were willing to relocate in exchange for a tax incentive. If the crown's normal collection of taxes from farmers was one-third of the agricultural produce, it might accept only one-sixth for the first five years, one-fourth for the next five years, and then back to the normal rate of one-third. The service providers such as apothecaries and barbers would receive, in addition to land, access to a captive customer base. The ruler benefited by having a developed territory where previously there was vacant land.

In 2023, India's prime minister was acting not much differently with a vision of turning a remote part of his home province of Gujarat into an unlikely center for manufacturing semiconductors. The *New York Times* reported that the government was offering about $10 billion in subsidies to fund 50% or even 70% of any company's outlay to compete in an industrial sector dominated by Taiwan.[23] The United States, concerned about reliance on high-tech imports from China, was starting its own heavily subsidized semiconductor manufacturing operations in Arizona.

The Chola dynasty way of integrating new territories into the ruler's domain has echoes today in what are sometimes called "special economic zones." China used this strategy to turn the small city of Shenzhen into a huge global center of technology, research, and manufacturing. Some of the most attractive areas of New York City, such as Manhattan's Chelsea Arts District, were developed in part through property tax abatements. Residents were attracted to revitalize decaying industrial or commercial zones by a promise that their new condominiums would have a property tax abatement that phased out over several years. Nongeographic communities have also won their share of tax alignment over the years, such as the nonprofit status granted to religious and veterans' groups. **So, the ordinary citizen can easily**

---

23   Alex Travelli, "Modi Wants to Make India a Chip-Making Superpower. Can He?" *New York Times*, September 13, 2023, https://www.nytimes.com/2023/09/13/business/india-semiconductors.html.

understand tax alignment, but that doesn't mean policymakers make the best use of the available strategies.

Policymakers too often passively receive development suggestions from their community and outside investors, a process that empowers the lobbyists who have the resources and motivation to promote special interests. Instead, policymakers should follow the methods by which business executives set their priorities. To borrow a device popularized by Steven R. Covey, categorize projects in these four quadrants: (1) Urgent and Important, (2) Not Urgent and Important, (3) Urgent and Not Important, and (4) Not Urgent and Not Important. Society should ideally focus on allocating or raising capital for that first quadrant, the urgent and important projects that must be funded right away, even if it means borrowing money. The second quadrant is open to voluntary contributions from citizens, either through charity or incentivized investment. **Just as good business leaders create and communicate a vision for their managers and workers, policymakers should, in Covey's often-quoted words, "start with the end in mind," and list the projects needed to get there.**

	URGENT	NOT URGENT
IMPORTANT	1	2
NOT IMPORTANT	3	4

A TOWERING EXAMPLE

The world's tallest building, the Burj Khalifa, opened in Dubai in 2010 after six years of construction. No community *needs* a 163-floor building, so you might say it was not urgent and not important. But it turned out to be a great investment because it helped fulfill the ruler's vision of making Dubai an international attraction, so what started as an oil-based economy was diversified into one based on high-end tourism, real estate, international finance, and commerce. The tower has a hotel, observation deck, offices, residences, and surrounding park, but just as important, it was designed to be a centerpiece for a community packed with new hotels, condominiums, and shopping malls. Building the Burj Khalifa required raising an enormous amount of capital, but the ecosystem it created has been quite profitable for the society.

Covering the Costs

When policymakers envision an infrastructure project aligned to society's needs, borrowing to raise the capital to fund it, they may not have difficulty repaying the debt. If they are building an ecosystem that benefits the society's entire economy, they can rely on tax collection. User fees may be an even better way to recoup the costs directly from those benefiting. In many cases, governments provide a service, such as a public library or park, but charge no fees because it is not traditional in that culture to do so. Or sometimes charging a small fee seems more trouble than it is worth. As modern technology makes it possible to go over a toll bridge or have parking validated by a merchant in an automatic, frictionless way, increasingly we will see how a usage tax can bring us first-class public facilities. The government can always distribute vouchers to ensure access or promote use by certain populations, such as students, seniors, or the indigent.

Taxation provides effective ways for policymakers to nudge both businesses and individuals to act in society's interest. An infrastructure project that is envisioned to be sustainable and to cater to the inhabitants begins with the end in mind.

Policymakers can offer incentives to ensure that the community's priority is funded, and if that goal aligns with an entrepreneur's business interests, it's a win-win. People in a community enjoy a sense of control over how the government is spending their money if they can contribute directly to a project. User fees such as road tolls offer the experience of direct contribution and can be used by policymakers to nudge people's behavior.

City-states including Dubai, Singapore, and Hong Kong are role models for using tax incentives to attract investment money for sustainable economic growth and development. Creating tax alignment is more challenging in some places than others, but societies can leverage technology and have regulators focus on promoting tax incentives as much as, or more than on enforcing tax collection.

While the potential benefits of tax alignment for businesses, individuals, and societies are clear, implementing these strategies is not without obstacles. As we move from theory to practice, it's crucial to understand the hurdles that may arise. In the next chapter, we'll examine the three most significant challenges to tax alignment and begin to explore how they can be overcome.

Takeaways for the Policymaker

- User fees, made increasingly efficient by technology, are an equitable way to fund society's needs and **are appealing to people** because **they feel a sense of control** over how the government is spending their money.

- People would welcome opportunities to get tax credits by making **voluntary contributions to projects close to their hearts.** Implemented systematically, these **contributions could grow to replace income taxes.**

- Tax incentives can be targeted not only to meet a community's urgent and important needs but also to promote economic growth by attracting investment and human resources.

PART III

Imagination

CHAPTER 6

The Three Challenges–*A Flawed System Lacks Trust and Awareness*

TAXES ENABLED ARE "EXPONENTIALLY" MORE VALUABLE THAN TAXES PAID

Suppose an entrepreneur reads about an enticing tax incentive described in a trade publication or newsletter. Usually, the writer will include a disclaimer advising the reader to check with their tax advisor. What happens next might go something like this: An entrepreneur we'll call Shyam, plans to import 50 high-end computers from Taiwan to India, where the import duty amounts to 40% of the computers' value. The government's motive for such high tax is to encourage consumers to buy a domestic product instead of an import, protectionism that is common around the world. Shyam has shopped around in India and believes his small but growing software development operation requires a level of quality and features found only in the imported product. He goes to his accountant and asks about some tax incentive he read about that might lessen the sting of the 40% import duty.

"Yes, you've got an export duty drawback incentive," the accountant explains.

Customs officials should rebate the import duty if the computers are used to produce goods that are exported at a value exceeding the drawback. Of course, there are conditions to be met and documents to be filed, and the drawback diminishes over time. The accountant nervously considers worst-case scenarios: Shyam receives the drawback but fails to market a competitive product and resells the computers domestically to pay his bills. Or the drawback expires before the value of the exported software exceeds the cost of the computers. Then there is the documentation problem. It's not like Shyam is buying auto parts and making cars that get shipped overseas with bills of lading. A revenue official might question the value Shyam claims on a software license he sells overseas.

"My friend," the accountant tells Shyam with a sigh, **"I assure you these incentives come with their own teeth, and they could bite you any moment in the future.** Unless you feel that the amount of this drawback can make a difference to you in the long run, I would request that you please don't take it."

How many entrepreneurs would be daring enough to reject such professional advice, even though it undermines the purpose of the tax incentive?

Considering the case we have made in the previous three chapters for seeking tax alignment, let's look at three main sets of challenges, starting with the mindset reflected in this fictional but realistic story about the duty drawback. Then we'll discuss the unavailability of authoritative information and, finally, how the execution of tax regulations creates a deep-seated bureaucratic resistance to alignment. First, a quick note to readers: **the United States has had duty drawbacks** since President George Washington signed the Tariff Act of 1789, and they still are underutilized.[24]

Challenge 1: The Mindset of Mutual Distrust

What word comes to mind when you think about the traditional relationship between the tax collector and the taxpayer? If your answer is *robbery*, while that may be a bit too strong a word, **the tax collector exists to extract money, and many taxpayers adopt an attitude that says, "I'm here to be exploited, and at your mercy, kind sir, because you have the entire state machinery at your disposal to make it happen."** This attitude constrains the entrepreneur who looks at tax only as an **obligation and never as an opportunity.** Regulators, meanwhile, **suspect that entrepreneurs are out to game the system, fleece the government, and amass wealth through immoral means.** When audits occur, distrust or perhaps hostility pervades the atmosphere on both sides. But there is a social contract to uphold in which taxpayer and tax collector should be reaching a fair payment agreement.

The taxpayer sees the government's thousands of pages of complex tax code and becomes absorbed with worry about not getting caught breaking any rules. Those pages are full of tax incentives waiting to be profited from, but the mindset of constraint keeps taxpayers from seeing the opportunities. And if they do see an opportunity, they will

> Those pages are full of tax incentives waiting to be profited from, but the mindset of constraint keeps taxpayers from seeing the opportunities.

---

24 "Tariff of 1789," FRASER: Discover Economic History, 3–4, https://fraser.stlouisfed. org/title/5884.

probably check with a tax accountant, who will immediately bring up regulations that might interfere. The same government whose lawmakers created the incentives discourages their use when it lacks a bureaucratic mechanism to work with taxpayers in a trusting, collaborative relationship. The entrepreneur sees only tax collectors who are single-mindedly intent on hunting down violators and assuming they are guilty until proven innocent.

The mindset must change in both directions. In our workplaces, we often see how collaboration rather than competition creates win-win situations, but somehow taxpayers feel locked into a win-lose relationship with the tax collector. Imagine if the tax collector said to the entrepreneur, "I'm here to help you grow your business," and the taxpayer understood that for the business to grow, a price must be paid to support the government's building of infrastructure and markets. **Around the world, there are instances in which this kind of cooperation occurs, even across borders.** One of the most prominent examples is Vietnam drawing huge investments from Singapore in recent years in many business sectors, including building industrial parks and technology infrastructure through special economic zones. This alignment results from the two nations having a trusting relationship, with Vietnam seeing Singapore as a stable and reliable partner, and Singapore being able to negotiate trade agreements with Vietnam that make tax regulations more transparent.

> Imagine if the tax collector said to the entrepreneur, "I'm here to help you grow your business," and the taxpayer understood that for the business to grow, a price must be paid to support the government's building of infrastructure and markets.

Challenge 2: Lack of Awareness, Access, and Certainty

The internet contains an overwhelming amount of data about tax incentives, but entrepreneurs have difficulty finding the exact information they need. No country, anywhere in the world, offers a single government database on the eligibility of tax incentives and benefits for businesses. In the United States, the Internal Revenue Service has struggled for decades to update its information technology. The archaic,[25] obsolete IT systems at the IRS have hurt its employee retention and kept it from being able to answer taxpayer questions in a timely way.[26] **Taxpayers rely on intermediaries, especially corporations that have lobbied the government to maintain a status quo that makes their tax preparation software indispensable to millions of users.** Other countries are far ahead of the United States at automating their revenue agencies' engagement process with the taxpayer. But even in countries such as India, where the government software is robust enough to compute the tax liability of individuals, that utility does not promote awareness of incentives or the ability of entrepreneurs to get clarity from regulators about how laws will be interpreted.

Let's say an entrepreneur is weighing business plans that could involve starting up an operation in or near Seattle, Chicago, or another US city. Even when businesses can find the information they seek from the IRS about federal tax benefits, where would they start to

---

25 "IRS Needs to Complete Modernization Plans and Fully Address Cloud Computing Requirements," US Government Accountability Office, January 12, 2023, https://www.gao.gov/products/gao-23-104719.

26 "Antiquated Technology Jeopardizes Current and Future Tax Administration, Impairing Both Taxpayer Service and Enforcement Efforts," 2020 Annual Report to Congress, US IRS Taxpayer Advocate Service, https://www.taxpayeradvocate.irs.gov/wp-content/uploads/2021/01/ARC20_MSP_06_ITmod.pdf.

search for the most relevant state and local tax benefits? DVS Advisory Group specializes in this type of investigation.

When tax regulations offer incentives, entrepreneurs often feel uncertain about whether, how much, or for how long they will benefit. An auditor could introduce a novel reinterpretation of a regulation. Regime change could upend a tax-alignment situation. Even the most stable democratic governments rewrite some laws and regulations from year to year, and a shift in the political balance of power can result in major changes.

If you are in the business of exporting software or IT services in India, the government offers you a slew of incentives. The industry has thousands of companies, large and small, and is a fast-growing driver of economic development in a country with 1.4 billion people. In researching India's Software Technology Parks incentive, we found that only about 980 software-exporting companies were claiming those incentives. When we asked client entrepreneurs about their reasons for not participating, the first thing we heard was that they were scared. **A typical question was "What if I take this incentive, and two years later they come back and say, 'No, you're not eligible'?"** The government would require that they pay back the incentive with a substantial penalty. Clients also said they found that the incentives came with conditions so onerous they were impractical. If they imported a computer for their export services, the government would waive the substantial customs duty. But they could use the computer only in one specified location and never for any domestic business. Executives of a fast-growing company with multiple locations don't have the mental bandwidth to remember these rules and inform the government every time they move a computer.

Challenge 3: Execution

Government regulators place onerous conditions on tax incentives to prevent false claims, even if that legalistic approach means expending resources out of proportion to the risk. The regulators focus their efforts on ensuring that nobody misuses an incentive, which as a result falls short of its potential benefit. **Undermining incentives with a bureaucratic mindset can send jobs or businesses away to competing countries,** as we have seen when Indian companies move operations to the Philippines. The easier the incentive is to claim, the more businesses will do so and the more impact it will have on the growth of an industry and its ecosystem of suppliers and other allied businesses.

> The easier the incentive is to claim, the more businesses will do so and the more impact it will have on the growth of an industry and its ecosystem of suppliers and other allied businesses.

Imagine if an index existed in which countries could be compared based on the ease of access to tax incentives. The metrics would be like the ones that jurisdictions cite to promote themselves based on ease of doing business. Many indicators go into the widely available rankings of countries showing which ones have business-friendly regulations. **What's missing is a metric on whether their tax incentives are accessible or hidden, whether those tax incentives are widely used or whether people are unaware or afraid to use them.** Regulators would be accountable for making the incentives available. Economies would grow faster and develop in the policymakers' desired directions as the incentives were better able to fulfill their potential.

Convincing government officials to surrender a portion of their power, even when it's for the common good, isn't easy. As we discussed in Chapter 3, historically, taxes were designed for reasons of security and control, to mobilize resources for the government, and to align public behavior, including, inter-alia, for funding the military. The prospect of jail terms or large fines hangs over people's consideration of claiming a little-known tax benefit. An individual regulator or auditor might disallow a tax incentive that appears to exist on paper. But the broader problem is that government sets the wrong vision for regulators, making them focus on rule enforcement, rather than ensuring that the incentives reach those eligible. Nations typically revise their tax laws every year and then delegate to their bureaucracies the development of operational rules and procedures. When issues arise about how to interpret the rules and procedures, the regulators issue circulars and notifications. Taxpayers must follow this steady stream of guidance, which they generally cannot challenge without a long, costly court fight. **The bureaucrats ultimately control the entire game, with the aim of checking misuse rather than enabling good use of the tax code.**

> The broader problem is that government sets the wrong vision for regulators, making them focus on rule enforcement, rather than ensuring that the incentives reach those eligible.

Government execution of its power of taxation can be uneven, and not just because of corruption or cronyism. In the United States, the IRS is aware for years that many of its wealthiest citizens repeatedly fail to file tax returns, counting on investigative and prosecutorial resource constraints to let them get away with saving billions of dollars. The IRS promised a crackdown after the chairman of the US Senate Committee on Finance urged the agency in a September 2023 letter "to significantly increase enforcement action against wealthy tax cheats who refuse to file tax returns."[27] The letter described the cheating as ongoing, brazen, and costing the US Treasury more than $65 billion over the four years since 2020. It said, "New data provided to the Committee by the IRS has identified staggering levels of noncompliance and criminality by high-income non-filers." News reports about this shortfall and about huge corporations paying little or no taxes may lead to a false image of the tax collector as weak in the knees when confronting influential and powerful people or enterprises. More accurately, **the tax collector is slow and deliberate when confronting the incredibly complex tax situations of the powerful.** For example, Microsoft revealed in a 2023 securities filing that the IRS had demanded $28.9 billion in back taxes, plus penalties and interest, after investigating how the corporation allocated its profits among countries and jurisdictions from 2004 to 2013.[28] The IRS audit of Microsoft began in 2007 and was one of the agency's largest ever.[29]

SORRY, WRONG NUMBER

In 2007, the British telecom giant Vodafone made what was then India's largest corporate acquisition and got hit with a surprise $2.2 billion tax bill, setting off a court case that was not resolved until 2012. The case reflected poorly on India as a place to do business because of bureaucratic overreach. Years earlier, the government of India had figured out a way to rake

27 US Senator Ron Wyden, Chairman, US Senate Committee on Finance, September 28, 2023, https://www.finance.senate.gov/imo/media/doc/wyden_letter_to_irs_on_high_income_nonfilers_final_092823.pdf.

28 "Microsoft Corporation," US Securities and Exchange Commission, October 11, 2023, https://www.sec.gov/ix?doc=/Archives/edgar/data/0000789019/000119312523254151/d530324d8k.htm.

29 "The IRS Says Microsoft May Owe about $29 Billion in Back Taxes. Microsoft Disagrees," Associated Press, October 12, 2023, https://apnews.com/article/microsoft-taxes-irs-96eb66abe86de19f1108209a8d57431a.

in needed foreign currency by waiving capital gains taxes on investments made by companies based in the Indian Ocean nation of Mauritius. Many American investors set up companies in Mauritius and had no capital gains taxes withheld on their investments in India. So, the Vodafone executives were gobsmacked when India's tax authorities denied a similar waiver on the acquisition by a Vodafone company based in the Netherlands seven months after it bought a majority stake in the India unit of Hutchison Telecom International, which was based in the Cayman Islands. Hutchison owned the India operations through a series of companies incorporated in Mauritius.[30] Basically, India's tax regulators were claiming that what Hutchison sold was a business asset in India, not shares of a Mauritius company. Eventually, the Supreme Court of India disagreed. Its ruling said, **"Tax policy certainty is crucial for taxpayers (including foreign investors) to make rational economic choices in the most efficient manner."**

Why It's So Challenging

Politicians are more motivated to create tax incentives than to follow through to make sure they are distributed fully and equitably. The incentives can be showcased to voters or financial supporters as part of a plan to address important issues, such as high

---

30 "Vodafone Wins $2Bn Hutchison Tax Case in SC," *Economic Times*, January 21, 2012, https://economictimes.indiatimes.com/industry/telecom/vodafone-wins-2-bn-hutchison-tax-case-in-sc-foreign-investors-cheer-historic-judgement/articleshow/11572738.cms.

unemployment or slow economic growth in a particular time or place. Once the incentives are adopted, implementation can be mired in bureaucracy. Regulators don't prioritize promoting the incentives, and tax collectors don't see it as their job to push anyone to take advantage. So, it's a pull mechanism in which the entrepreneur must figure out what strings to pull. But first, the entrepreneur must become aware that the business is eligible for the incentive. Second, we have self-constraint because traditionally, we have been told that tax is something you pay, not a place to look for opportunities to make money. And third, the entrepreneur must overcome the fear that ambiguous regulations have created a trap in which taking the benefit will result in legal problems or at least painful compliance steps.

The lack of awareness and difficulty of access are less of a challenge for multinational corporations, which can hire former bureaucrats who know what incentives are available and how to get the most out of them. Even if there are no incentives, they understand the government's policy objectives and how to ask for favors within the framework of law. The inability of small or midlevel entrepreneurs to have similar awareness, access, and certainty does not serve the common good. Their start-up or disruptive enterprise might be just the right player to address the issue for which the incentive was created. Suppose, for example, that a small pharmaceutical enterprise is working on a breakthrough that threatens to undercut Big Pharma's established business in a multibillion-dollar healthcare spending area such as cancer treatment. Society would benefit from incentivizing investors to support the small player if only it had access to the same regulatory levers controlled by Big Pharma.

TAX SOMETIMES HITS THE WRONG TARGET

A businessman in downtown Vancouver, Canada, received a surprise tax bill of nearly CA$17,000 in 2019 for having an empty home—the town house where he was operating his marketing agency. The bizarre explanation for his quandary is an extreme example of the challenges of alignment. Lawmakers in Shawn Moore's province, British Columbia, created what they called a speculation and vacancy tax to address a crisis in afford- able housing. The goal was to discourage speculators from outside the area, including overseas, from buying up homes in a fast-rising market and leaving them empty. The province promised to apply the tax revenue to building more affordable housing. Vancouver had a similar empty homes tax already, so its residents were covered by both taxes.

According to news reports in 2019, Moore had lived and worked for several years in the town house he owned, which was zoned by Vancouver for residences, offices, or a combina- tion of both. As his business grew, he bought another home downtown to live in. He still spent the night occasionally in the town house occupied by his agency until the business outgrew it and moved elsewhere, and he rented it out to another business. That was in the year Moore got audited by provincial tax authorities. Although the empty homes tax was a municipal levy, the city deferred to provincial regulations that defined the town house for the purpose of that law as residen- tial, because people legally could live there. And nobody was living there once Moore declared his new home as his primary residence.[31] These tax laws ensnared some unintended targets, people who were forced to spend time and money trying to prove they were not speculators. After five years, though, the laws were mostly seen as successful in significantly reducing the vacant home problem.

Even when tax benefits are local, a lack of awareness is possible, as I learned from a friend who produces beer in Milwaukee, a midwestern US city best known for its long history as a hub for breweries. He was shocked to find out from a vendor manufacturing company that he was eligible to tap incentives related to the city's promotion of jobs and economic activity. The manufacturer's representative had discovered that other microbreweries he did business with didn't know about the tax incentive and took it upon himself to spread the word.

Knowing about an incentive is just the first step in execution for taxpayers who must determine whether it applies to them and whether they are prepared to claim it. They need to understand how the government department that gives the incentive operates. Will the business have to provide so much information and be subject to so much supervision that the incentive is not worth the trouble? Another concern is that the regulation that includes the incentive may carry compliance requirements that are set out in other laws or regulations. For example, an export incentive might require compliance with a law that manages foreign currency exchange, and that law could have its own set of rules for exporters.

---

31   Rafferty Baker, "Vancouver Man Gets Surprise $17K Bill for Empty Homes Tax on Live-Work Townhouse," CBC News, June 26, 2019, https://www.cbc.ca/news/canada/british-columbia/vancouver-empty-homes-tax-live-work-property-1.5190203.

If the incentive comes with timetables for compliance, it's important to know what workarounds or appeals are possible in the real-world situation in which a deadline can't be met.

Getting Professional Help

Because no tax incentive happens independently, it pays to seek professional assistance before claiming a benefit. A professional who specializes in tax alignment can advise about the context in which the incentive should be understood, and what steps must be taken, and in what order. If a business will not owe duty on an import because it will be exported later, must it pay a withholding tax in the meantime? The answer is, it depends. Entrepreneurs are eligible for more tax incentives than they take because they don't know what questions to ask or where to get the answers. The best place to start is with a professional firm that has experience with complex transactions in the relevant jurisdictions. At DVS Advisors, we explain to our clients the benefits and the risks involved so they can make an informed decision. Taking risks is in the DNA of entrepreneurs, so if they know what they are getting themselves into, they are prepared to assume the consequences.

The wording of tax regulations can be daunting even on the common forms that business owners file regularly. **When tax codes run thousands of pages, it's impossible for a human being to never violate a provision.** Is that mobile phone or car really being exclusively used for business as you claimed? The revenue agency won't know if your spouse calls that phone and asks you to stop on your way home to pick up some groceries in that car. We know what leeway we give ourselves when following the letter of the law seems impractical, and that we are unlikely to be challenged on our actions. But business tax incentives carry higher stakes; **too often they are worded ambiguously, often intentionally, and are more likely to be subject to formal interpretation—and reinterpretation in court rulings.** Suppose your business takes a federal incentive without incident, but a bureaucrat in a different state refuses a similar usage there, in a decision upheld by a court ruling. The government can then reopen your account and ask you for a refund of whatever benefit you received. In other cases, **courts in different states make contradictory rulings, a situation that feeds the fear and uncertainty surrounding tax alignment.**

While the intent of this book is to encourage businesses to profit from tax alignment for the betterment of society, not to sow fear of missing out or suffering unintended consequences, it was necessary in this chapter to caution entrepreneurs about the challenges that must be understood and overcome. Taxation is **steeped in a mindset in which the collector focuses on revenue goals and taxpayers and tax advisors worry more about compliance than creating opportunities to profit.** The complexity of taxation and the lack of resources governments devote to providing clarity about their sometimes-shifting interpretations of tax law make it daunting to find and seize an opportunity for alignment. And finally, the execution of tax benefits focuses on rule enforcement by the government and compliance by the taxpayer, not on ensuring that the incentives reach those eligible.

> The complexity of taxation and the lack of resources governments devote to providing clarity about their sometimes-shifting interpretations of tax law make it daunting to find and seize an opportunity for alignment.

Despite these formidable challenges, the **potential rewards of tax alignment make it worth pursuing solutions.** In fact, each obstacle **we've identified presents an opportunity for innovation and growth.** As we turn to the next chapter, we'll explore practical, actionable solutions that can transform these challenges into stepping stones towards a more efficient, equitable, and prosperous tax system.

CHAPTER 7

The Three Solutions–*We Can Overcome Each of the Big Challenges*

[

WHEN YOU BEGIN WITH ALIGNMENT,

SUCCESS IS A SHARED VISION

]

The news media used many superlatives to describe the success of Mundra Port on the 25th anniversary of its 1998 opening in Gujarat, India. It had become the nation's largest, most efficient seaport, and it handled the most container traffic. It was the heart of the Adani Group conglomerate, and reflected the visionary leadership of Gautam Adani, one of the richest men in Asia. Adani, a college dropout, was in his midthirties when he made an offer to the Gujarat government to convert marshlands into a port. He gave the government a 26% share in exchange for funding and concessions, which eventually included a huge surrounding special economic zone, a classic example of alignment, and not Adani's first. He was still in his twenties in 1991 when he took advantage of Indian government worries about not having enough foreign exchange to buy oil. The government offered enormous incentives for exporters, so Adani began exporting whatever he could get his hands on, from pin to plane. Adani deposited foreign currency income that filled government coffers, and in turn his bank gave him his proceeds in rupees and the government gave him waivers called "scripts" to import items that normally would be banned from import. Adani profited by selling those scripts to people who needed them in India. Then he went back to the foreign markets to figure out what else he could export to keep the win-win cycle going.

I began reading a biography of Adani midway through writing this book about tax alignment, expecting to find examples in his career. What I also found was that when he first listed his company at merely 32 years old, he was already frequently saying, **"We must align ourselves to national priorities,"** resonating with the premise of this book. He said there was a business opportunity and a national need, and **"when both get aligned, the tide itself upholds the swimmer."**[32] A stunning example of Adani aligning himself with government goals is taking shape in what is expected to be the world's largest renewable energy plant. Adani Green Energy Limited is building the Khavda solar power plant on barren land in Gujarat five times the size of Paris. At this writing, 2 GW has already been operationalized by Adani Green Energy Limited (AGEL) of what is expected to be 30 GW from solar panels and wind turbines. The government, which has a goal of achieving 500 GW of nonfossil fuel capacity by 2030, provided notable tax breaks on the plant's transmission of electricity and depreciation of its machinery.

Adani was far from the first industrialist to build upon national priorities, as American magnates John D. Rockefeller did with oil, Andrew Carnegie with steel, and Cornelius Vanderbilt with railroads

---

32 R. N. Bhaskar, *Gautam Adani: Reimagining Business in India and the World* (Penguin Random House India, 2022), 71.

in the 19th century. What makes these magnates exceptional is the energy, effort, and courage they put into achieving alignment, because governments do not make it easy. Corporate tax laws invariably are written to facilitate collection, not to make compliance smoother for the taxpayer. **The billionaires who have the most spectacular success aligning their businesses with the nation's priorities often generate a mix of admiration, suspicion, and social criticism.**

For those entrepreneurs who are not billionaires walking the corridors of power, a strategy of alignment seems daunting—not because of outside criticism but because of their own fears or lack of knowledge. This chapter will discuss some solutions for each of the three biggest challenges to alignment, so entrepreneurs can become aware of opportunities and avoid being warned off by skittish financial advisors.

Solution 1: Mindset of Possibility

Whether or not they realize it, entrepreneurs benefit from strong tax regulations. Most entrepreneurs want to see their businesses expand and their profits increase over time, growth that requires the government to keep the economy and markets in shape. It doesn't happen by itself without good regulators. The virtuous cycle goes like this: **If the regulator is strong, the market is strong. If the market is strong, the entrepreneur has a much better way to thrive and make money.** And then, the entrepreneurs should have no problem paying a fair share of taxes, assuming the tax has predictability, certainty, and finality. They understand that the government needs the resources to build a better society.

The challenge comes when multiple layers of laws and regulations from different jurisdictions and agencies cause so much complexity that noncompliance seems inevitable. If the tax collector is seen as a predator waiting for the prey to make a wrong move, the resulting anxiety saps entrepreneurs' innovation and creativity.

The **Mindset of Possibility** requires a collaborative climate in which the entrepreneur and the regulator feel that "We are both in it together." **Only by working as partners can they fulfill the potential of creating the best market with the most possible revenue for both entrepreneur and tax collector.** For entrepreneurs to be creative and successful, regulations must be enabling. When the regulator has only enforcement as a goal, business owners chafe and waste time and energy fighting to free themselves from what they consider oppressive rules. Enabling by regulations happens in many situations, especially in the more developed economies, and its spread should be encouraged.

A government's tax authorities do not act in isolation from that jurisdiction's legal establishment, including how all its laws are enforced in business and financial matters and its economic climate. Tax is the consequence of a series of activities: someone sets up and operates a company, finds a market, makes some money, and decides whether to take out profits or reinvest in the business and its workforce. Tax is the consequence of that journey. Ideally, the government is enabling from the start, making it quick and easy to set up a business. In Singapore, not coincidentally one of the few governments that operates with a budget surplus, you can set up a company in four hours and have all your tax IDs and other paperwork set in two days. This process takes weeks, if not months, in the United States or in India. Multinational corporations are used to transferring their people around the world, and they can do that with entities and contracts too. They will put a holding company in Singapore for its regulatory certainty, base a contract in London for its acceptable arbitration rules, and have a US operating company for the American market opportunity.

LIKE SINGAPORE OR LONDON—ALMOST

We had an American client that was dealing with an Indian company, and both parties decided to have their contracts written so that any arbitration would happen in Singapore. It was expensive to do it that way, but the client knew enforcement of the law would be fair and unambiguous. Now India has taken a lesson from Singapore and Hong Kong by establishing the Gujarat International Finance Tech-City, or GIFT City, as a place for multinational corporations to have a base, which was established in the prime minister's home state. The vision is to have an international financial services center that applies global best practices of regulation and is as comfortable for these corporations as London. Despite initial challenges in mindsets and complexities in prevailing regulations, India offered tax exemptions, regulatory shield, and subsidized property sales in what was barren land up until then. The result: GIFT City boasts almost all the world's A-list multinationals and has created billions of dollars of trade flows, which otherwise would have happened elsewhere in the world. GIFT City has become a hub for expats and a foreign destination within India for businesses to escape domestic regulations, and the journey has just begun.

Solution 2: Platform of Alignment

The alignment challenge requires the government to be more forthcoming about how it is using taxation to elicit desirable behaviors from its people and businesses. For our clients, DVS Advisory Group has started collecting, in a user-friendly database, the possibilities for alignment. Ideally, a digital **Platform of Alignment** should be publicly available showing what governments need and how ordinary citizens and entrepreneurs can have their tax obligation discharged by matching what they naturally want to support. **Incentivize these contributions, and taxes will be transformed from a collection process to a fulfilling game of alignment.**

Modern monetary theory provides a rationale for creating such a platform at sufficient scale to make a real difference in our national economies. The theory, which we discuss briefly below, is explained well by Stephanie Kelton in the best-selling 2020 book *The Deficit Myth: Modern Monetary Theory and the Birth of the People's Economy.* The book expands on often-argued concerns about national budget deficits to look at the political changes necessary to responsibly use available resources.[33] If this approach takes off, the world will be a completely different and better place.

Criticism of deficit spending reached a crescendo in the United States and other countries after the COVID-19 pandemic disruptions of the world economy led to massive government stimulus programs. The critics said governments printing money without restraint were fueling inflation and burdening future generations with debt. Modern monetary theory's response is that federal governments are not like your household or your business because they

---

33   Stephanie Kelton, *The Deficit Myth: Modern Monetary Theory and the Birth of the People's Economy* (New York: PublicAffairs, Hachette Book Group, 2020).

can print money. **A government whose debt is in its own currency, as is the case for the United States, doesn't need taxation to pay its bills.** Unlike when currencies were backed by gold, the government can easily add a couple of zeroes to the one-dollar bill. Regulators must keep inflation in check, but the economy can absorb a reasonable amount of inflation when federal policy protects consumer spending and investment capacity. **Governments have not proven themselves to be efficient allocators or utilizers of capital, and when they collect more tax revenue to repay external debt, they suck up purchasing power in the market, leaving the economy less capacity for growth.** When governments leave more money in circulation, then according to monetary theory, consumption and economic growth will increase.

Embracing modern monetary theory can free us of worries about saddling future generations with debt. It changes our focus from measuring whether spending exceeds tax revenue to measuring all the resources we have or could create. Countries whose debt is not borrowed in foreign currency are monetarily sovereign. When China holds US treasury bonds, the American government is in debt to China but could print the money to repay that debt. In our digital age, it could be done with the click of a button. Most developed nations have monetary sovereignty. Some developing nations have low debt because they have low economic activity, but among those borrowing for growth, such as India, foreign currency debt is mostly under control. There are worrisome exceptions such as Venezuela, that get a lot of attention due to hyperinflation. But when inflation is in check, debt concerns should not be a driver of tax policy. We should think about taxation in the terms we discussed in Chapter 3 regarding its potential to mobilize resources and meet society's needs, including by aligning public behavior.

Our work at DVS Advisory Group involves researching tax incentives for our clients, and we are bringing what we discover together to make it easier to search. You could say we are building a platform for tax alignment, but the fact remains that searching the world for possibilities remains a huge challenge. No platform exists in any country, excluding certain city-states, that allows an entrepreneur to search all the tax incentives available from central and state governments. No mechanism exists to fully answer the simple question "How can I align my business with the government's needs and desired behaviors?"

Governments know how to create a **Platform of Alignment**. A classic example involves the US military, which ended its draft more than 50 years ago and relies on the continuous recruitment of volunteers. Recruiters make it a matter of pride and patriotism to join, and they offer incentives such as educational and healthcare benefits, as well as immigration benefits (naturalization). Government employees have it as their job to publicize and explain the benefits, to devise strategies to address recruiting shortfalls, and to emphasize that joining is a matter of pride. Private corporations and the public frequently reinforce the government's culture of rewarding veterans and service members. Those on active duty are told they can board an airplane ahead of others and are thanked for their service. That recognition happens even when their service involves preparing citizens of another nation to fight a proxy war or performing a mission the public has no idea how to explain.

Enticing the public to contribute constructively to build a market economy should be easier than persuading young people to risk their lives in the military. The government could build a platform that lists major projects that need funding. It could document and display projects to replace bridges that have exceeded their lifespan and become unsafe or extend broadband to rural areas where schoolchildren don't have internet access. Politicians know what projects like these are needed. Instead of having to sell the project to colleagues in a legislative body's backroom deal, they would be marketing them directly to taxpayers with details, including cost, displayed openly. If the marketing is effective, revenue automatically starts flowing in. Corporations and other interested parties would help with the marketing, redirecting campaign contribution money from politicians to projects that serve the common good. **The process would give citizens more control and insight into how government spending and public behavior are aligned. Bad things happen when tax money goes into a giant pot where people have a very limited view of how it is spent and feel a lack of control.** The wealthiest people dodge taxes, sometimes even by moving to another country. Entrepreneurs stay out of certain markets where they could have created needed economic growth.

A **Platform of Alignment** would grow naturally over time and enrich society. Governments probably would exempt most of their budget items from such public control at first, based on various rationales. Policymakers would argue that some spending was already mandated, some was too arcane to explain, and some had to be kept secret for national security reasons. But even if the platform started with 20% of the budget, public pressure would cause it to expand significantly over time. Nobody enjoys the task in which they learn how much tax they are paying each year. Now imagine that the undertaking begins with a fulfilling ritual in which the taxpayer chooses to contribute to pet projects on the **Platform of Alignment**. The platform then grants credit for those contributions and displays a large drop in the taxpayer's remaining rate. Sheer joy—or, to put it more scientifically, a flow of oxytocin and serotonin—would result, feeding a desire among taxpayers for more contribution options. **People like contributing to a cause. It brings them together in a sense of community.**

FUELING DEBATE OR DRIVING BUSINESS?

In Chapter 6 we discussed how most societies pay for maintaining roads by taxing the price of our car, fuel, or annual vehicle registration combined with user fees that include tolls based on distance traveled, bridges and tunnels traversed, and truck weights. The small city-state of Dubai did well with tolls, but in a large state or nation, a **Platform of Alignment** would be a more scalable and equitable solution. California has nearly 40 million people and more than 175,000 miles (about 285,000 kilometers) of public roads.[34] It's common knowledge that California has the highest fuel prices among the continental US states and that a major factor is the confusing array of direct and indirect taxes. When Californians fuel up a vehicle, they would be hard pressed to know what part of the bill goes to taxes and what portions of that tax support roads and bridges or reducing greenhouse gas emissions. Periodically, a spike in prices or a proposal to increase or repeal one of the taxes prompts heated debate. Lately, critics of the taxes have focused on equity issues: low-income workers pay a distressing share of their wages for gas, especially when forced to move far from their jobs to find affordable housing. Wealthier people can afford electric cars and pay no gas tax. What if the road and bridge projects were on a **Platform of Alignment** rather than dependent on fuel station payments? Transportation and logistics companies, car dealerships, and others

---

34 "State Transportation by the Numbers," US Bureau of Transportation Statistics, accessed October 19, 2023, https://www.bts.gov/browse-statistical-products-and-data/state-transportation-statistics/state-transportation-numbers.

interested in road maintenance would eagerly contribute in exchange for tax credits and public recognition. You would see billboards or advertisements at the fuel stations in which the companies tout their contributions as a point of pride and a way to drive more business.

A **Platform of Alignment** would draw interest from the whole socioeconomic spectrum, including our wealthiest citizens. In 2010, the American billionaires Warren Buffet and Bill Gates announced The Giving Pledge to encourage philanthropy among the world's wealthiest people. Hundreds of billions of dollars of charitable spending have been pledged, but without requirements on when or how they would be spent. **Tying this giving to annual tax credits and funneling it into government-sanctioned programs would make for a more timely and dependable way to fund the billionaires' passion projects.** Some philanthropists give away their wealth slowly during their lifetimes or delay major donations until after their death. Gates was retired from running Microsoft and Buffett was nearly 80 years old when they announced The Giving Pledge. Our current tax systems encourage self-serving and inefficient mechanisms, as major donors set up foundations or programs and hire staff to research and administer their giving.[35] A **Platform of Alignment** could coordinate and better direct the

> Everybody has passions they are willing to support, and the government should be the enabler.

---

35   This concept is explored further in the bestseller by Anand Giridharadas, *Winners Take All: The Elite Charade of Changing the World* (New York: Alfred A. Knopf, 2018).

spending. Everybody has passions they are willing to support, and the government should be the enabler.

Solution 3: The Taxpayer as a Customer

A government's revenue service should operate more like a business for reasons that are becoming more compelling as globalization gains speed and takes on new forms. A tax collector who says, "I'm here to collect taxes," has a myopic way of looking at the enterprise of fulfilling the purposes of taxation. **In taxation, the more we pay, the more we feel submissive and vulnerable, the opposite of the business world's rewarding its best customers with better service, more attention, and lower fees.** Business operators selling you a ticket for a show, a tour, or a flight know they are selling you an experience, and they don't convey the attitude, "I'm here only to collect money." Even if the transaction is happening online, a business markets the value, convenience, and rewards of the experience it is selling. The goal is to engage customers in such a way that they don't mind paying. If the experience is going to be painful, people look for a way out, which is exactly what happens with taxation. Some of the wealthiest citizens have fled countries or states to escape tax regimes they despise.

Countries with the most-developed economies have been working for years through their G20 and Organisation for Economic Co-operation and Development groups to deal with tax avoidance by multinational corporations. When these companies shift profits to lower-tax jurisdictions, they erode the tax base of the higher-tax jurisdictions, which have responded with what they call a two-pillar solution. Basically, pillar one began to address how globalization and digitalization allowed companies to artificially shift profits internationally to exploit differences in tax laws. Pillar two aimed to create a global minimum corporate tax rate. Unfortunately, **by the time the bureaucrats huddle at their conferences to grapple with their differences and try to understand the magnitude of the problem, it is already evolving beyond the reach of their "solutions."** For example, consider the delay in governments reacting to the rise of cryptocurrencies that made it impossible to trace who owns what. Or consider the lagging government actions to protect personal data from theft and misuse. Entrepreneurs are adept at envisioning future opportunities to exploit. When paranoia sets in among policymakers because they have lost control of an issue such as cybercurrency or data protection, they often overreact with draconian regulations that are impractical to enforce. So, the **tax authorities' only way to succeed is to collaborate with entrepreneurs.**

If regulators embraced what we have called the **Mindset of Possibility** and set out to build a **Platform of Alignment**, taxpayers would see the government being transparent about its needs and spending plans. Transparency builds trust, and when trust is built, no one has a problem giving, especially the wealthy. That statement may be hard for some people to believe, but it is well grounded in psychology. The psychologist Abraham Maslow famously

> Transparency builds trust, and when trust is built, no one has a problem giving, especially the wealthy.

theorized in the 1940s that human needs fall in a hierarchy in which behavior is driven first by physiological needs such as food, water, and shelter, and then by safety. Once those basic needs are mostly met, human behavior is motivated by love and belonging. In Maslow's influential hierarchy of needs, esteem is the second highest of the five motivations, and self-actualization is the highest. Feeling good about yourself and being recognized by others are high-level motivations that a **Platform of Alignment** fulfills for those of us fortunate enough in life to benefit from treatment of the taxpayer as a customer. When people get rich, they search for social validation and the fulfillment that comes from contributions to society.

If we open our minds to the idea that the role of government is to enable and not to control, then regulators should focus on helping the market thrive and grow. We have a rueful saying in my country that China grows because of the government and India grows despite the government, though there has been a remarkable improvement in this scenario over the past decade thanks to determined leadership and alignment of bureaucracy with national priorities. In most developing countries, **the biggest challenge is that regulators feel a need to control because they fear losing control.** In highly developed countries, regulators become complacent, even as prosperity degenerates into high income inequality and social divisions. As the investor Ray Dalio warned in his 2021 best-selling book, the result can be civil war.[36] A **Platform of Alignment** is the best way to ensure that countries stay in the era of prosperity by putting their wealth to good use rather than having it shifted to lower tax jurisdictions. It's increasingly easy for people of means to move from one part of the world to another. In the 2022 e-book *The Network State: How to Start a New Country*, investor Balaji Srinivasan envisions national boundaries ceasing to exist, replaced by digital communi-

> A **Platform of Alignment** is the best way to ensure that countries stay in the era of prosperity by putting their wealth to good use rather than having it shifted to lower tax jurisdictions.

---

36   Ray Dalio, *Principles for Dealing with the Changing World Order: Why Nations Succeed and Fail* (New York: Avid Reader Press / Simon & Schuster, 2021).

ties.[37] That future seems plausible enough that current governments have an existential need to open their minds to treating the taxpayers as customers and looking for opportunities to collaborate with them.

> For those interested in exploring tax-alignment opportunities or contributing their expertise, taxasprofit.ai aims to be a centralized resource and community. This platform represents a step toward the future we've envisioned, where tax-incentive information is readily accessible and continuously updated by a global network of professionals and stakeholders.

We have seen in this chapter that entrepreneurs need strong but clear regulation in a system that is collaborative and enabling. Everybody benefits if taxpayers can grasp the possibilities for their alignment with government priorities. **Worries about whether a government is spending more than it is collecting in revenue have overshadowed the potential of responsible uses of available resources to incentivize and promote economic growth.** Giving taxpayers a platform to find incentives to align their interests with the government's needs would help businesses fulfill their tax obligations in a way that benefits the public good and spurs market growth. People hate paying taxes to fund spending they don't control, but they enjoy contributing to society. By treating the taxpayer as a customer, a government can engage its people in a rewarding

> People hate paying taxes to fund spending they don't control, but they enjoy contributing to society.

37 Balaji Srinivasan, *The Network State: How to Start a New Country* (self-published e-book, 2022), https://thenetworkstate.com/book/tns.pdf.

community experience. Entrepreneurs have long ago found ways to shift profits and avoid high-tax jurisdictions, a problem that expands with globalization and digitalization. Those same forces can be integrated into new systems of tax alignment.

With these solutions in mind, we stand on the threshold of a transformative shift in how we perceive and interact with taxation. As we move into our final chapter, let's dare to imagine a future where tax alignment is fully realized. **In this vision, taxation evolves from a burden into a powerful tool for positive change, seamlessly integrated into our collective efforts to build a better world.** Join me as we explore this exciting possibility and its far-reaching implications for businesses, individuals, and societies around the globe.

FIND THE BEST PLACE TO BUILD YOUR NEXT VENTURE

Scan the QR code below to explore *The Great Places to Build, Finder*—our dynamic dashboard ranking the most attractie geographies for entrepreneurs, based on policy, tax alignment, and ease of doing business.

CHAPTER 8

Freedom and Prosperity–*Tax Alignment Can Change Our World for the Better*

[

REALIZATION PRECEDES REFORM.

]

Imagine we are in the future and looking back at the 2030s, which commentators sometimes called the Age of the New City-State. The term did not refer to the kind of city-states that developed naturally on islands like Singapore and Hong Kong. These new city-states were more like the Mundra Port in Gujarat, India, that we discussed in the previous chapter—the product of alignment between national leaders and visionary entrepreneurs.

The most prominent example was Neom, which was launched in 2017 by Saudi crown prince Mohammed bin Salman as a $500 billion development intended to diversify the country's oil-based economy with an environmentally conscious planned city. It was envisioned as a hub for luxury tourism on the Red Sea and in the Sarwat Mountains and for trade, manufacturing, agriculture, and the development of renewable resources. The Saudi leader's futuristic vision and execution of the project had plenty of critics, and skeptics questioned how investors, tourists, and millions of new residents could be drawn to the desert of northwest Saudi Arabia. As with GIFT City, Neom had a catchy four-letter name. Both projects benefited greatly from the assurance of government sponsorship as a "special economic zone" with independent regulation and tax concessions. Neom was presented as offering freedom and a unique culture very different from the image that Saudi Arabia had internationally. These projects seemed exceptional, but even in their times, they were not pioneering examples of tax alignment. In India, the huge Reliance Industries refinery and petrochemical complex completed in 2000 in Jamnagar, Gujarat, expanded to become the world's largest oil-refining hub[38] and accounted for 55% of total special economic zone exports from India.[39]

Around the same time that Neom launched, Silicon Valley billionaires began covertly buying up land in a mostly agricultural region northeast of San Francisco to create a new city. The investors not only lacked government sponsorship, but also kept policymakers in the dark for years about what they were doing and ran into resistance from potential sellers.[40] Prospects of fulfilling the developers' vision also ran into the bureaucratic and political barriers typical of the United States, especially in California, where major projects drag on for years, beset by lawsuits and cost overruns. A project like this one

---

38   "Expansion Makes Jamnagar the World's Largest Oil-Refining Hub," Bechtel, corporate impact report accessed June 12, 2024, https://www.bechtel.com/projects/jamnagar-oil-refinery.

39   "RIL's Jamnagar SEZ Contributes 83% to the State's SEZ Exports," *Economic Times*, June 23, 2012, https://economictimes.indiatimes.com/news/economy/foreign-trade/rils-jamnagar-sez-contributes-83-to-the-states-sez-exports/articleshow/14356785.cms.

40   Conor Dougherty and Erin Griffith, "The Silicon Valley Elite Who Want to Build a City from Scratch," *New York Times*, updated August 28, 2023, https://www.nytimes.com/2023/08/25/business/land-purchases-solano-county.html.

in the San Francisco Bay Area would require political support for rezoning agricultural land for housing, studies and hearings on environmental impact, and millions of dollars spent to win an enabling ballot initiative. Meanwhile, companies drifted away from Silicon Valley because of California's unusually high taxes.

The new city-states like Neom and GIFT City that aligned their vision with the needs of their government and the desires of their investors have attracted the money, talent, and skilled labor to become successful hubs. Each of these states have their own identity and character. What they shared was a willingness to create airports or seaports, or both, with huge capacity before it was needed. As envisioned in the 2011 book *Aerotropolis: The Way We'll Live Next*,[41] the growth of an ecosystem around an airport, even if built in the middle of nowhere, replaced the old model of placing an airport on a city's outskirts. The government did not have to build the core infrastructure but did act as an enabler in drawing private investment. **The unique identity and culture of the city-state did not have to be universally loved but only needed to be attractive to enough people.** The attractions were futuristic architecture, cutting-edge technology, lifestyle benefits, and—last, but not least—**tax policies and incentives.**

Nations Become Service Providers

Predicting the future is always risky, and this chapter's foretelling assumes that we cast aside Industrial Age concepts of what determines whether a nation is developing or developed. **We are moving into a time when the developed countries will be those whose**

---

41   John D. Kasarta and Greg Lindsay, *Aerotropolis: The Way We'll Live Next* (New York: Farrar, Straus and Giroux, 2011).

governments build systems to measure the economic impact of businesses. Those nations will have the enabling infrastructure we discussed in the previous chapter on solutions to the challenges of alignment. Their governments will understand that their role is to set the framework for contribution and recognition. Their role is not to build, own, and operate the infrastructure but to enable others to do so. Nations become service providers. They will attract entrepreneurs aligned with their government priorities, and their markets will thrive and grow.

In this future vision, *nations don't choose taxpayers; taxpayers choose governments.* Businesses and individuals will choose where they want to pay their taxes based on what they are going to get in exchange. That kind of social contractual arrangement is not that big a stretch from current reality, in which tax policymakers are scrambling to catch up as corporations and individuals can relocate with more speed and less friction than ever. In April 2020, India enacted an equalization levy to indirectly tax cross-border e-commerce. Such moves to have businesses pay taxes based on where their customers are from, reflect how irrelevant the domicile of a business has become. US companies register in Nevada or Delaware, even if that's not where they do business.

> We are moving into a time when the developed countries will be those whose governments build systems to measure the economic impact of businesses.

Governments will operate as infrastructure enablers the way hotel corporations enable franchise holders. Marriott International, Hilton, and other big hotel corporations primarily are marketing their brands and making rules for management at properties owned by others. Except for some marquee properties that the big hoteliers own as a matter of corporate pride or for their real estate value, their business is managing the framework of engagement with vendors and customers for the actual hotel owners, which may be smaller businesses or real estate investment trusts. These owners choose which hotel corporation and brand they affiliate with, and sometimes when a contract expires, one side or another decides to change partners. Likewise, governments of the future will have to compete for the affiliation of infrastructure investors.

The Indian government has pioneered the public-private partnership model for large-scale road and airport infrastructure projects. The government benefits by having a private concessionaire raise funds for construction from institutional lenders. But before taking bids for such a concession, the government must assess whether the project has commercial viability. In technical terms, is the project's internal rate of return greater than its weighted average cost of capital? A highway improvement project might have a clearly identifiable revenue stream if the concessionaire was able to collect a predetermined toll from projected traffic over a certain number of years to cover financing costs. But even if the commercial viability of the project falls short, the government might justify providing incentives to private partners based on an appraisal of the project's economic benefits. The improved highway might have fewer accidents or lead to the establishment of business and commerce that creates jobs.

As businesses adopt tax-alignment strategies, the positive impacts can extend far beyond the balance sheet. **When companies thrive through smart tax alignment, they create jobs, invest in communities, and contribute to overall social and economic prosperity.** This in turn can lead to better-funded public services, improved infrastructure, and enhanced quality of life for families and communities.

Moreover, as entrepreneurs demonstrate the benefits of tax alignment, they can inspire broader societal shifts. Imagine a future where individuals, like businesses, can more easily align their personal contributions with societal needs they're passionate about. This could lead to more-engaged citizenship and more effective use of public resources.

Mobility Will Force Changes

There is no reason to believe that taxation won't evolve from its present forms. As we discussed in Chapter 3, **taxation dates to the time when people were hunter-gatherers and shared with their tribes.** The development of agriculture led to larger colonies and eventually kingdoms, states, and nations, each with their own formal tax systems. But that structure is not sustainable. **With the amount of mobility we now have in terms of capital, talent, and markets, we don't need to be operating a business in our place of birth, operation, or domicile. We could operate it from anywhere or nowhere.** A **global digital company** of the future will envision itself as located on planet Earth, domiciled in any data server or multiple data servers simultaneously, and the practical way for it to contribute what we now call taxes will be through the domicile of the customer consuming its goods or services. *Taxation has been adapting gradually to e-commerce and our ability to buy financial assets and digital services from anywhere, but eventually tax must be entirely consumer centric.* The technology of the Information Age and the shifting supply chains that affect product provenance make it

> A **global digital company** of the future will envision itself as located on planet Earth, domiciled in any data server or multiple data servers simultaneously, and the practical way for it to contribute what we now call taxes will be through the domicile of the customer consuming its goods or services.

increasingly difficult to establish the provider's domicile. **Current nations will collect contributions (taxes) based on their ability to attract consumers, who will be able to move about the world at ever-increasing speeds.** Today we have air travel, but something much faster, such as the hyperloop, is inevitable.

Unless governments make it attractive for people to stay where they are, mobility will increase. Some sectors such as farming will remain more tied to geography, but a lot more people will shop for the best domicile the way some corporations register in the Cayman Islands or very wealthy Europeans put their money in Swiss banks. Archaic laws will have to change to catch up with this new reality, a process that will be most challenging for the large governments. They will become like landlords who have gotten comfortable collecting high rents on property that no one wants to lease anymore. Currently, an American citizen living anywhere in the world must pay US taxes on foreign income, after certain exemptions and credits.[42] Future generations in a more mobile world are not likely to accept that kind of law. The number of Americans applying for a second citizenship is relatively small but growing. They qualify based on their descent or their ability to buy a "golden passport" by investing in countries such as Türkiye, Portugal, or the UAE.

Desire for Freedom Will Prevail

Some jurisdictions already have value-added taxes based on what is consumed in a particular market, but in a more seamless future world, additional solutions will emerge to address the mobility of

---

42   "LaHood Introduces Bill to Modernize Tax System for Americans Living Overseas," Congressman Darin LaHood, December 18, 2024, https://lahood.house.gov/2024/12/lahood-introduces-bill-to-modernize-tax-system-for-americans-living-overseas.

people, goods, and services. **Although the world will continue to have physical territories, there may be global tax pools.** People or businesses would be domiciled based **not on a physical location but by their digital real estate.** This concept is not much different from any international organization that exists through voluntary contributions. Young Presidents' Organization and Entrepreneurs' Organization, organizations for founders, entrepreneurs, and chief executives that I belong to, have more than 40,000 members in over 150 countries, each contributing a substantial amount of money to create a mutually beneficial community experience. DVS was a part of the World Economic Forum, where we discuss the challenges of our times and set the global agenda of the future. We contribute not only to get value from networking, learning, and personal development but also because, by working together, we can create programs to make the world a better place for our families, companies, and employees. *The Network State* e-book, mentioned in the previous chapter, explains in depth how attracting people to networks could be scaled up to "a large enough population, income, and real-estate footprint to attain a measure of diplomatic recognition."[43]

Technology and precedent exist for scaling up a digital network independent of nations, as we have seen when blockchain allowed people to create currencies recognized internationally. The rise of cryptocurrencies showed that **mass acceptance is the only thing that matters in giving a currency value. Ultimately, a currency is a medium of exchange that is acceptable to people on scale.** If people believe that a particular currency has value, whether it is digital or a physical piece of gold or silver, then it has value. Multiple factors

---

43 Balaji Srinivasan, *The Network State* (e-book in which each section is online as a separate webpage), https://thenetworkstate.com/the-network-state-in-one-sentence.

can drive the acceptance; The military and economic might of the United States helps ensure the value of the American dollar as a reserve currency worldwide. The desire for freedom drives the acceptance of cryptocurrency among people who want to build their own controls and processes. Regulators prefer to have a central bank to monitor transactions, but watching central banks print money undermines the trust in what's behind that currency. In a few years, crypto grew from a curiosity unknown to most people to something that about a billion people had used, proving popular willingness to embrace decentralized alternatives to established institutions. Crypto will continue to evolve, and in some future form it will play a big role in overcoming the challenges to tax alignment.

Another effect we have seen with digital platforms is how easily they enable crowdfunding, which solicits contributions based on an emotional appeal. **Fear is the main emotion countries use to get people, especially entrepreneurs and ultra-high-net-worth individuals (UHNIs), to pay taxes. When taxpayers are treated like customers, their status in their jurisdiction will rise with their payments. And countries will use the emotions of respect and pride to keep entrepreneurs and UHNIs in their territory.** Instead of simply paying taxes, they will enjoy the freedom to contribute for designated purposes listed by the government. What we will call contributions and the value-added tax on the facilities the government offers will soon make up 80% of a country's revenue. Consumption tax will expand and be used to fund what we will call the SCE mandate,

When taxpayers are treated like customers, their status in their jurisdiction will rise with their payments. And countries will use the emotions of respect and pride to keep entrepreneurs and UHNIs in their territory.

the programs the government requires for **safety, certainty, and empowerment**. In other words, the government would have that consumption tax revenue for purposes like paying the salaries of regulators, judiciary, etc.—basic functions that nobody would be eager to contribute to.

The main roles of the government will be providing internal and external security and setting a framework for contribution, regulation, and recognition, making the system predictable. Examples of a government providing predictability include securities regulation and civil courts where businesses can sue to enforce contracts or file for bankruptcy protection. **By establishing empowerment mechanisms for the population to contribute toward a thriving nation, the government will enable alignment.** In turn, businesses will have the option to choose between the best infrastructure providers for work and the best market opportunities for serving. This concept is not far removed from what is already happening. The disruption of the highly regulated taxi industry gave us the Uber driver, an independent contractor who can choose where to work. This driver may live in one city for lifestyle reasons but choose to work somewhere else, not too far away, where the roads are better, operating a car is cheaper, and customers are plentiful.

Sources of Innovation Will Shift

The most-developed nations such as the United States led the world in technological innovation through the end of the 20th century, but have fallen behind in areas crucial to tax alignment, which is why we have been discussing a seaport in India and could be looking at Dubai or Türkiye to offer the biggest airport. The younger nations or city-states have the same characteristics that we see in first-generation entrepreneurs. They have nothing to lose. The old guard G7 nations have everything to lose and spend their energy protecting their bastion rather than confronting new challenges. Their focus is on preserving the world order and blocking inevitable change, or at least using their bureaucracy to delay it. It is noteworthy to mention that the GDP of the 5 developing BRICS countries, have surpassed that of the developed G7 nations in 2020.[44]

The ways in which the emerging states outpace big powers like the United States may seem small but will give them a serious competitive edge. One way is how they facilitate business travel—quickly approving new direct flights to accommodate changing needs and getting international travelers through their airports quickly. The last time I landed at JFK International in New York City, it took me two-and-a-half hours to get out of the airport. In Dubai, I can pick up my checked luggage and reach the taxi terminal within five minutes of leaving the plane. If that seems unbelievable, you are out of touch with how the hungry emerging states are innovating. They will also have a competitive edge if businesspeople feel safe from crime there, as they do in Dubai, Singapore, or Hong Kong, cities where the shoplifting sprees and car thefts seen in cities like San Francisco are unimaginable. Meanwhile, the United States has too many graduates leaving college with huge student loans, which causes anxiety that kills innovation. The generations that are taking two or three decades to pay off student loans are a drag on the economy that can't be fixed without foundational reforms. America has great resources but, as noted earlier, maintains a military budget greater than the next 10 countries combined, allocating its revenue in ways that don't meet

---

44   MG Chandrakanth, "HOW BRICS Countries Have Overtaken the G7 in GDP Based on Ppps," Times of India Voices, April 9, 2023, https://timesofindia.indiatimes.com/blogs/economic-policy/how-brics-countries-have-overtaken-the-g7-in-gdp-based-on-ppps/.

its people's needs. The private sector owns phenomenal digital infrastructure, while the government and the bureaucracy lag badly, except in terms of military and intelligence infrastructure. As one example, India issued a digital certificate for the COVID-19 vaccination, while the US federal government relied on paper certificates.

Throughout history, the world map has changed significantly, so it should not be surprising when city-states emerge, that offer digital domicile to people and companies unaffiliated with any nation. Being a citizen of planet Earth will be as natural as it is today for someone to identify as Indian, American, or Sri Lankan. Compared with the tedious, plodding systems governments have used to control migration in the past, the new regimes will be as convenient as a hop-on, hop-off bus tour. For those invested in this type of freedom, having it as an option will be life changing. Some won't be interested in the new mobility, but they will still enjoy a spillover effect from the resulting competition. **As choice of domicile becomes more readily available and convenient, governments will start treating citizens with a lot more respect.**

Taxation Will Be Democratized

As the emergence of digital domiciles shifts control from the regulator to the taxpayer, governments will be forced to consider the overall tax impact of businesses and entrepreneurs. **Companies that fuel the economic engine and create jobs will be systematically rewarded with tax incentives and investment subsidies in recognition of the multiplier effect,** resulting from their paying wages and buying goods and services. An entrepreneur who makes $1 million in profit feels fleeced paying an income tax on that amount without being credited to some extent for the several million dollars of resulting taxes the government takes in from its suppliers and employees, and from their income and consumption. **Digital domicile will allow entrepreneurs to choose governments that value their tax impact as the contribution to society that it really is.** The tax incentives will spread around the world in the same way programs grew at the beginning of the 21st century to encourage sustainable energy, and carbon credits are issued to discourage emissions that cause climate change.

Let's use a fictitious example to show how businesses can be measured on the extent of tax flow they've been able to generate in the economy. Chennai Ottowerks is an engineering services company that makes a component for German luxury cars in India. The German automaker contracts with Ottowerks to fill orders valued at $10 million on an annualized basis. Ottowerks charges an additional 18%, or $1.8 million, in Goods and Services Tax (GST), which goes straight to the government of India. To fulfill the order, Ottowerks must buy $8 million worth of equipment on which it pays an 18% value-added tax. Its costs also include $400,000 in rent, utilities, and various other administrative expenses, which are subject to various GST rates of 15% to 18%. Ottowerks pays $1 million in salaries and wages, of which $200,000 goes to the government, because the employees owe an average of 20% in income taxes. To keep the math simple, let's say the employees put $100,000 of their net income into savings and spend the remaining $700,000. Again, the government gets an 18% GST on the employees' consumption.

If you sum up these transactions, Ottowerks cleared $600,000 in pre-tax profit (30%) and helped the government with the tax flow of $1.8 million on its sales and another $1.8 million-plus on the resulting income and value-added taxes. The scenario in which Ottowerks earned only 6% profit is realistic because a German luxury automaker would have enough prospective suppliers to be able to drive a hard bargain on the contract. **The tax revenue was six times larger than the profit, and that doesn't even include the multiplier effect down the line as the suppliers and employees pay GST on their spending.** As a result, the government could afford to make some concessions to keep the next contract from going elsewhere.

ENTITY	NET REVENUE	TAX PAID	
Ottowerks auto contract	$10,000,000	$1,800,000	
Parts and equipment suppliers	$8,000,000	$1,440,000	
Overhead expenditures	$400,000	$60,000	(at a 15% minimum rate)
Salaries and wages	$1,000,000	$200,000	
Ottowerks profit	**$600,000**	$180,000	
Employee spending	**$700,000**	**$126,000**	
Total tax flow		**$3,806,000**	

Note: *Tax on parts and equipment suppliers is eligible for input credit. It is still relevant for computing tax flows, as higher tax flows create higher tax bases, which in turn lead to higher collection and lower evasion.*

The Tax Multiplier Effect

We need a new way to evaluate business contribution that reflects how the creation of tax flow varies by industry. Economists generally say that one dollar spent in the real estate sector creates economic value of three or four dollars. That multiplier effect is easy to envision for anyone who has sunk money into furnishing and maintaining a new home. Governments will create benchmarks like this for each sector, and their tax systems will include subsidies or credits rewarding businesses for their larger tax impact. Each sector will have safe harbor rules, so businesses will not have to submit detailed calculations proving their tax impact unless they choose to. Entrepreneurs will have an incentive to start businesses in sectors that have a higher tax impact on the local economy. **Governments will get more-transparent and higher-quality revenue as a result, with no more burden than regulators are already used to in making systems to categorize materials for cross-border taxation as goods move around the world.**

Digital Systems Will Prevail

Government collection of financial data will be digitized in a way citizens of some countries have never seen. In the United States, private companies, including those that provide software for tax preparation, have managed to keep the government from stream-lining tax filing. The US Internal Revenue Service has information technology that government inspectors have called antiquated. In India, by contrast, we are used to the government capturing data on where even small businesses take in and spend their money. Under the One Nation, One Tax reform enacted in 2016 in India, all the consumption taxes fall into a single federal database. The program eliminated inefficiencies and paperwork from 30 states plus other jurisdictions, all having separate and different tax rules and filing procedures. Businesses serving the nation of 1.4 billion people could ship goods from one end to the other without having checkpoints or separate warehouses for tax purposes. The reform eliminated the need for state tax IDs. Even better, it significantly reduced tax evasion and lowered the government's tax administration costs, resulting in lower tax rates. Today, the corporate tax rate for India is about 22%, one of the lowest in the world.

Eventually all taxpayers will use a government portal to create their tax invoice electronically. They will simply have to enter their unique identifier, which in India is a 12-digit number called Aadhaar. India already requires larger businesses to use the government's tax portal to issue their invoices to their customers, so the government has full transparency into the impact of a business. The main benefit for entrepreneurs is predictability, as they automatically pay taxes monthly and have no year-end surprises. A more efficient system also lowers their overhead costs and makes it easier to document their loan-worthiness for banks. Previously, entrepreneurs in India who kept poor tax records had to borrow at high interest rates from private moneylenders. Of course, even the most efficient system won't prevent the challenges created by overly aggressive bureaucrats, who will have access to more data than ever. But the increased transparency of going digital—documents on a government portal and hearings with remote officials on recorded videoconferences—puts the taxpayer on a more equal footing. There can be no backdating of documents or signatures and no misstating of what was said or received.

Developing countries and new city-states that build efficient digital infrastructure will leapfrog established world powers when it comes to the ability to measure the impact of businesses on the economy. Most of the countries we consider developed based on their GDP per capita, not just the United States, will have to catch up to compete. The evidence can be seen in the multimillion-dollar rise in foreign direct investment in India in the years since the One Nation, One Tax reform was implemented. That is a clear measure of the investor confidence in the new systems.

Magnets for Investment

Entrepreneurs are attracted to jurisdictions that have sped up the pace and reduced the complexity of government interactions for businesses, particularly when tax incentives are involved. As recounted in chapter 6, Vietnam set up special economic zones in partnership with Singapore. These zones are managed as a commercial corporation by Singapore, which makes them magnets for entrepreneurs. They get the efficiency of Singapore in a country that is one-third the cost of Singapore, and with tax-friendly terms. Textile manufacturing businesses across the world have moved there.

We had a client making high-end clothes for the European market in a joint venture with a Hong Kong–based company that wanted to expand its operations in India. Having an alternate location to manufacture and export was a priority, to reduce the risk that a geographically limiting challenge in the supply chain would hurt the company's operations. Also, the client had received a large order for fast fashion from a multibillion-dollar European brand. Those big operators employ the toughest negotiators, who squeeze their suppliers for low prices. Our client had to expand operations while finding lower land prices and bringing down its labor costs. The client explored a less expensive country in South Asia first, and then we suggested Vietnam. Both governments offered tax incentives, and Vietnam would have lost out if cost had been the only consideration. When we weighed the pros and cons and mentioned Singapore's reputation of efficiency and predictability, the client settled on expanding into one of Vietnam's special economic zones.

Entrepreneurs of the future will be drawn to jurisdictions that have digital platforms like India's that make taxes more predictable and enable the government to measure the total tax impact of a business. The jurisdictions that offer incentives based on that impact will become magnets for investment. Businesses that contribute value to the society and the economy will have that impact recognized in lieu of any net tax collection. Tax won't even seem like a relevant word for their contributions. The slower-moving developed democracies will be compelled to match the digital data–driven incentives that are attracting entrepreneurs elsewhere.

> The jurisdictions that offer incentives based on that impact will become magnets for investment.

CONCLUSION

A Bedtime Story of the Future

[*IMAGINATION IS YOUR INHERITANCE*]

We have described a future in which governments do not expect tax payments from those who make equivalent contributions to society and the economy based on their passions. It all starts with governments creating digital platforms capable of capturing in real time the transactions happening in their economy. Businesses will be able to use these platforms to obtain data-driven incentives as they contribute to causes prioritized by the government. Entrepreneurs will be attracted to the jurisdictions that develop these digital platforms and frameworks with more transparency, convenience, and predictability than their competitors offer. In an increasingly mobile world, people will consider themselves citizens of planet Earth and demand the freedom to choose their digital domiciles unrestrained by national or state boundaries.

In this future, I imagine having grandchildren blissfully unaware of income tax. This is how a conversation with them would transpire:

Divakar (Grandpa): Dear children, have you ever heard of this concept called income tax?

Sanjana Jr. (granddaughter): What is that, Grandpa? I've heard of the concept called tax as something we pay when we buy stuff.

Sanjay Jr. (grandson): I believe income is something we earn for doing work, but what is income tax?

Divakar: Well, every time you earn income, you had to pay a share to the government.

Sanjay Jr.: Really? But why should I pay a share to the government? It was my effort that earned the income.

Divakar: I agree, Sanjay, but how do you think all the roads you travel on are built, or the police who provide security or the courts that function are paid for?

Sanjana Jr.: Don't we make contributions toward those?

Sanjay Jr.: I think I've seen billboards of people who helped fund the bridges and public buildings.

Divakar: Yes, dear, but many years ago, a couple of decades back, we had this concept called income tax. A portion of our income was paid to the government.

Sanjana Jr.: Then who decided how to use that money?

Divakar: The government decided where to spend it.

Sanjana Jr.: How could the government decide that? They sit in one part of the country and decide how things need to be spent in every district and state?

Divakar: Yes, dear, that's how the system used to be.

Sanjana Jr.: But isn't that unfair?

Divakar: I'm not sure if it was unfair. Maybe it was the best methodology we knew at that time.

Sanjay Jr.: So, you had this concept called income tax?

Divakar: Yes, but now we don't have income tax. We have voluntary and mandatory contributions.

Sanjana Jr.: Wow, I can't imagine a world where people were forced to pay tax without knowing how that money would be spent.

Divakar: I agree. That was an era where the government's role was to collect and allocate funds.

Sanjay Jr.: So, what is the government's role today, Grandpa?

Divakar: Today, the government's role is more about being an enabler. They build the channels for us to engage.

Sanjana Jr.: Nice. So how do you think the future is going to be?

Divakar: No idea—that's for you people to imagine. This was a future we imagined and reimagined, moving on from some archaic practices.

Sanjay Jr.: How about common citizens being made responsible to collect and deploy taxes and contributions?

Sanjana Jr.: We should be allowed to pay our taxes in kind … like, if I am an engineer, I can contribute my time to the government instead of paying taxes.

Divakar: Probably that could become a possibility when you reimagine the scenario.

Sanjana Jr.: Is it even possible?

Divakar: Of course, dear. You are only limited by your imagination, and imagination makes us infinite. Now, let's sleep. Good night, darling.

Sanjay Jr. and Sanjana Jr.: Good night, Grandpa.

Moving On …

This book is a deep dive into the way governments take and allocate a share of the value created by their people. Historically, we saw how taxes had three main purposes: **mobilizing resources, redistributing income, and aligning public behavior.** Focusing on that last purpose, pushing people to behave in certain ways allowed us to envision tax as an opportunity and not as a cost. We have seen how people, especially entrepreneurs, anywhere in the world can adapt this mindset—**tax as an opportunity**—**to benefit by devising strategies to align themselves, or align their business or community, with the government's needs.** Doing so requires solving three main challenges. A **Mindset of Possibility** is necessary to overcome the mutual distrust in the relationship that governments and their tax collectors have traditionally established with their people. Using a different approach, creating a **Platform of Alignment** and treating the **taxpayer as a customer,** governments could engage their people to stop seeing taxes as a burden. I have optimistically predicted that this tax-alignment philosophy will lead to a brighter and perhaps world-changing future. In the meantime, entrepreneurs can create their own **Mindset of Possibility** and begin looking for alignment opportunities.

To learn more about tax-alignment opportunities or to contribute your expertise to a global community, visit taxasprofit.ai. Together, we can work toward a future where taxation becomes a tool for mutual benefit rather than a burden.

AFTERWORD

AI and Beyond—*The World of Taxation, Transformed Forever*

EVOLUTION MAKES THE IMPOSSIBLE INEVITABLE

When I began writing this book nearly a two years ago, the word "AI" didn't appear once in my manuscript. It wasn't oversight—it simply hadn't permeated my professional lens with the clarity and urgency it commands today. But as I approach this closing chapter, it's impossible to ignore how profoundly the landscape is shifting. We are no longer in an era of gradual evolution; we are in the midst of a seismic transition. Perhaps even a transformation. The contours of the future are dissolving boundaries we once assumed were permanent—national, economic, and professional.

We are entering an age where agents—autonomous AI executors—will become the new actors in commerce, law, and even diplomacy. Agent-to-agent interactions will replace traditional transactions. The velocity of economic exchange will explode, and the world will feel increasingly borderless. Customers and creators alike may be domicile-less; the very idea of origin and destination—long foundational to taxation—will blur beyond recognition. Expertise will no longer travel through people; it will be cloned, distributed, and deployed through machines. The human race will be infinitely mobile, not by movement, but by replication of thought. In this age, a single expert—or influencer, or creator—can spawn billion-dollar ventures at scale, not by scaling themselves, but by scaling their digital proxies.

Landscape Ahead

As we move into this AI-native era, the foundations of commerce, regulation, and value creation are shifting in ways that traditional systems are not prepared for. The world of taxation, in particular, stands at a critical crossroads. Below are three defining shifts that will characterize the new landscape:

- **Agent-to-Agent Transactions Will Redefine Scale and Speed**

  Autonomous AI agents will conduct economic activity with a level of efficiency and volume that surpasses human limits. These agents won't just assist; they will initiate, negotiate, and execute transactions. Tax authorities will face the daunting task of understanding interactions between entities that are neither human nor easily attributable.

- **Domicile Will Become Fluid, If Not Obsolete**

  As customers, creators, and businesses operate through distributed digital identities, the concept of domicile—so central to tax residency and jurisdiction—will lose its meaning. When both the buyer and seller are digital agents operating in cloud-native environments, which country claims the tax? The lines will blur irreversibly.

- **Expertise Will Be Cloned, Scaled, and Monetized Globally**

  A single expert's knowledge can now be turned into a thousand intelligent agents, each solving, advising, or transacting across geographies. This means the barriers to scaling knowledge work vanish. A two-percent elite of creators and experts could shape multi-billion-dollar digital economies—without hiring, relocating, or even traveling.

What Will Change

As we look ahead, three fundamental shifts will redefine the nature of work, value, and structure in the AI-driven, borderless economy:

- **Who We Engage With**

  In a world mediated by intelligent agents, our engagements will increasingly be with systems rather than people. Customers, vendors, collaborators—even regulators— may be represented by AI proxies. Identity will become fluid. Reputation systems, digital signatures, and real-time verification layers will matter more than passports or physical addresses.

- **What We Value**

  Value will migrate away from effort and hours to outcomes. The traditional model of charging for time, presence, or even process will fade. What will command value is unique insight, originality, emotional resonance, or influence—all of which can be scaled exponentially through digital products or platforms. *"Chargeable time" will be replaced by "deployable intelligence."*

- **Whom We Employ**

  Employment will no longer mean hiring people. **It will mean orchestrating ecosystems**—AI agents, human freelancers, APIs, and micro-service nodes across jurisdictions. The very notion of a company will shift from being a collection of employees to being a network of interoperable capabilities. Entrepreneurs won't scale teams, they will scale systems.

What Will Stay

Yet amid this transformation, some principles remain remarkably constant—anchoring us through the turbulence of change:

- **Taxes**

  Governments will still need taxes to function—but how they levy and collect them will evolve. In a decentralized, fast-moving world, ***tax policy will have to shift from control to coordination, from enforcement to integration.*** While the instruments may change, the need for revenue remains immutable.

- **Trust**

  In a world of bots, deepfakes, and autonomous agents, trust will become even more critical. Systems, brands, and individuals that can establish trust—transparently and repeatedly—will dominate.

- **Alignment**

  The central argument of this book remains true: alignment is everything. But here's the pivot—*historically, entrepreneurs were asked to align with societal needs. In the future, societies will need to align with entrepreneurs.* Nations, cities, and governments will compete to attract the best entrepreneurial talent.

The Challenge for Regulators

Regulation at a Breaking Point: If entrepreneurs are evolving at the speed of code, regulators are still moving at the pace of paperwork. This gap will widen—and with it, a fundamental tension. Regulators will struggle to keep pace, and the instinctive response in many mature economies may be to clamp down. *When evolution lags, enforcement becomes the fallback.*

Rise of Policy Magnets: Regulators who choose to become enablers rather than enforcers will win—and win big. The opportunity lies in designing frameworks that attract innovation rather than repel it. The age of regulatory centralization is fading. In its place, newer, smaller societies—both physical and digital—will rise. Estonia, for instance, already offers e-residency to global entrepreneurs. City-states, nimble island nations, and even forward-thinking subnational regions will compete not on land or labor, but on policy, trust, and ease of doing business.

Rise of Digital Nations: Meanwhile, large tech platforms are fast becoming the pseudo-nations of our time, wielding outsized influence not just economically, but socially and politically. With billions of users, their decisions can shape speech, commerce, and behavior at planetary scale. And yet, they remain largely outside the purview of conventional regulation. Eventually, we may see some of them attaining potential sovereignty.

The World of Taxation: 2030 and Beyond

By 2030, the global tax landscape will look nothing like it does today. Destination-based taxation will accelerate, but defining "destination" in a digital, agent-led world will remain a stubborn puzzle. Consumption-based taxes will thrive, offering governments a visible, enforceable, and politically palatable model.

Citizens will demand more control over where their taxes go. The idea of a toll-based economy—where tax becomes a transactional choice tied to services received—will gain momentum. The public will no longer accept vague promises in return for opaque tax burdens. Governments will be challenged not just to collect, but to justify. Value attribution, once the bedrock of tax logic, will become nearly impossible to trace. In this new reality, servers, not borders, may determine value creation and tax residency. And more importantly, the opportunity for alignment will determine a geography's success.

A Future Worth Watching

As the world tilts into a future filled with complexity, speed, and boundless possibility, the call to align has never been more urgent— or more exciting. ***Alignment will no longer be a theoretical ideal.***

It will be the single most strategic lever—binding entrepreneurs, societies, and governments into a shared journey of value creation.

Some regions will get this right—and they will thrive. Others will resist the change—and watch their talent, capital, and creativity migrate toward more enabling environments. *We are no longer asking where the world is headed. We are asking who will be ready when it arrives.*

And as someone who has spent two decades witnessing the ever-evolving dance between state and enterprise, I can only say this: it is fascinating to imagine. And I truly can't wait to see it unfold.

I thank you, my fellow traveler for taking this journey with me, I had a truly fulfilling and exciting time exploring the mystic world of taxation together, and I hope this is just the beginning.....

Until we meet next time.....

Divakar Vijayasarathy
20th June 2025

I've distilled my entire learning into **five principles and seven frameworks** that help you understand, master and structure taxes globally.

If you'd like to explore these further, simply **scan the QR code** to access the *Tax as Profit Mastery Program.*

ACKNOWLEDGMENTS

This book would not have been possible without the unwavering support, encouragement, and contributions of many wonderful people in my life.

First and foremost, my deepest gratitude goes to my wife, Kavitha, who has been my true pillar of strength. Her belief in this work, her constant motivation, and her steady presence made it possible for this book to find its way into the world. Without her, this would have remained just an idea.

To my daughter, Sanjana, I owe a special thanks for her extraordinary patience and meticulous attention in proofreading the manuscript—multiple times, at that. Her care and dedication have shaped this book in more ways than I can count.

I am especially grateful to Ms. Turirya Uma Kalyan for her analytical support and constant feedback across multiple topics throughout the book. Her insights added depth and nuance to several key sections.

To my incredible team at DVS—Sundararajan K, Subhash Renganathan, Viswanath D., and Sridhoola Skandraaj—thank you for standing by this project from the beginning. Your contributions in editing, research, and proofing were instrumental in bringing this manuscript to life. A special thanks to my secretary Emmel Manlapaz for his tireless coordination

I am also grateful to Mr. Pradeep Chakravorty, author and historian, whose unique perspectives informed and enriched several parts of this work.

A heartfelt thanks to Adam Witty, CEO of Forbes Books and his incredible team Patti Boysen, Shandi Thompson, Katie Smith, Megan Elger, Ruthie Wood, Howard Goldberg, and Jenna Panzella, for believing in this vision and supporting it every step of the way.

To each of you—thank you for walking this journey with me.